Sacred Space Of Healing

Set In Soul

This Journal Belongs To

_____

Dedicated To Not Letting What Tried To Damage Us Control Us.

Table Of Contents

How To Use This Journal   6

My Experiences   7

A Piece Of The Past   22

Because It Is Getting Better   52

How To Use This Journal

Coping with trauma is not easy. You constantly struggle with negative emotions. You feel upset and helpless and you're frequently distressed by tension, anxiety, and memories that refuse to go away. You feel hopeless, depressed, angry, and terrified. You feel shame and guilt, blaming yourself for what has happened. You are often edgy. You can't sleep. You can't concentrate. Your heart races. You feel tense, both physically and emotionally. Everything seems to leave you afraid and disconnected. You withdraw from other people – even from family and close friends who mean well. You don't think you can get over the pain, trust anyone, or feel happy or safe again.

This journal is designed to help you cope and heal. By using this journal, you make use of what therapists call 'the process of expressive journaling.' This enables you to express yourself and possibly heal from the trauma. When you repress or inhibit your feelings or thoughts, you allow them to fester and weaken your physical and emotional well-being. By doing this, you then develop long-term stress and anxiety. When you face up to the experience as well as to the emotions it creates, you put the experience in its proper perspective. You open yourself up to healing.

This journal helps you release pent-up feelings about your traumatic experience. Use this journal to pour out what happened to you. Articulate your thoughts and emotions. Don't hold back. Feel free to express your thoughts and feelings without the fear of being judged. You're writing for yourself. Do not pretend. Do not restrain yourself. Embrace your feelings. Express everything that is within your mind and heart as this allows healing to take place. Writing freely will help release the buildup of negative feelings. It helps you to go deep down to the root of the pain and confront it. It helps you to process the pain. It is often difficult to confront a traumatic experience; however, braving through the pain creates a pathway for healing. It clears the clutter. It liberates you. It allows you to forgive others and it allows you to forgive yourself. It also allows you to let go and to learn acceptance.

We recommend using this journal every night to reflect. Doing this helps you to understand and make sense of your experience. It helps you to derive meaning. It teaches you what to do next to heal and recover from the experience. Take your time when you write in your journal. Look for a peaceful and quiet corner. Be conscious about slowing down. Think about writing as a means to catch your breath from constantly thinking about your trauma. Create a sense of stillness and peace. Be mindful. Using a journal this way gives you strength and hope. It gives you a sense of purpose. It gives you the courage to move forward. It makes you realize that you are capable of healing. It also makes you realize that you have the potential to rise above your experiences and conquer any storm that life brings. This is your sacred space of healing so let's get started.

My Experiences

A Traumatic Experience For Me....

A Traumatic Experience For Me....

A Traumatic Experience For Me....

A Traumatic Experience For Me....

A Traumatic Experience For Me....

A Traumatic Experience For Me....

A Traumatic Experience For Me....

A Traumatic Experience For Me....

A Traumatic Experience For Me....

A Traumatic Experience For Me....

What Do All Of My Traumatic Experiences Have In Common?

What Issues Do I Want To Address?

What Issues Am I Not Addressing?

What Issues Do I Need To Address?

A Piece Of The Past

A Piece Of The Past

What Are Some Important Personal Events That Have Happened In My Past (List Good And Bad)?

A Piece Of The Past

A Traumatic Event That Has Happened To Me That Still Affects Me Today:

How Long Have I Been Dealing With This Trauma?

What Are Some Replayed Thoughts?

What Triggers A Memory Of Any Of My Traumatic Events?

When I Experience A Flashback Of A Traumatic Event, I:

A Piece Of The Past

How Do I Feel About People Associated To The Trauma?

How Do I React To People Who Trigger My Trauma?

My Response To A Trigger:

How Do I Feel About Places And Activities Associated To The Trauma?

What Are The Negative Thoughts I Have About Myself?

A Piece Of The Past

Do I Experience Feelings Of Anger, Fear And/Or Guilt Towards The Trauma?

If I Responded Yes To The Previous Prompt, Why?

Do I Feel Scared?

If I Responded Yes To The Previous Prompt, What Am I Scared Of And Why?

What Is PTSD?

A Piece Of The Past

Do I Feel Ashamed About Anything?

If I Responded Yes To The Previous Prompt, What Am I Ashamed Of And Why Am I Ashamed Of It?

I Have Always Viewed Myself:

I Would Like To View Myself:

An Internal Struggle For Me:

A Piece Of The Past

Do I Blame Myself For What Happened?

I Have Been Avoiding:

What Happens When I Do Not Address Something That Hurts Me?

I Have Been Hoping _____ Goes Away.

How Do I Manage My Emotions?

A Piece Of The Past

What Am I Worried About?

What Are My Needs?

I Feel Like It Is Selfish Of Me To:

Do I Get Anxious?

If I Responded Yes To The Previous Prompt, What Do I Get Anxious About?

A Piece Of The Past

What Causes Me To Shut Down?

What Are Some Of My Deeply Held Beliefs?

Who Do I Trust?

Why Do I Trust The Person/People I Mentioned In The Previous Prompt?

Do I Believe I Am Currently In The Process Of Healing?

A Piece Of The Past

If I Responded Yes To The Previous Prompt, Do I Believe My Healing Is Taking Too Long?

If I Responded Yes To The Previous Prompt, Why Do I Believe It Is Taking Too Long?

If I Believe My Healing Is Taking Too Long, Am I The Reason Why?

Do I Believe There Is A Certain Time Frame To Heal From This Trauma?

Have I Ever Tried To Heal On My Own From This Trauma?

A Piece Of The Past

If I Responded Yes To The Previous Prompt, What Have I Done To Try To Heal On My Own?

Do I Trust Myself?

How Do I Protect Myself?

I Feel Powerless When It Comes To:

I View The World:

A Piece Of The Past

What Do I Feel Like My Experience/s Meant?

I Want To Become:

I Cannot Seem To Control:

I Would Like To Regain Control Of:

My Purpose Is:

A Piece Of The Past

My Goals Are:

Do I Feel Helpless?

Do I Often Feel Stressed?

What Contributes To My Stress?

I Have Witnessed Someone:

A Piece Of The Past

I Found Out:

I Have Been Exposed To:

My Loved Ones Have Been Exposed To:

I Feel Disconnected From:

Now I Feel Connected To:

A Piece Of The Past

I Have Lost:

Changes Within Myself That I Have Experienced Since The Trauma:

The Impact That This Trauma Has Had On My Body:

What Do I Feel Like Is Not Real?

I Space Out When:

A Piece Of The Past

Nightmares I Have Had:

Moods I Have Experienced:

Negative Thoughts I Have Had:

My Heart Rages When:

What Is Expected Of Me?

A Piece Of The Past

What Is It That I Cannot Live Up To:

Based On My Response To The Previous Prompt, Answer The Following: Why Do I Believe That I Cannot Live Up That? Who Expects Me To Live Up To That? Do I Want To Live Up To That? When Will I Stop Trying To Live Up To That? How Does It Make Me Feel To Not Live Up To That?

I Know That With Help, I:

How Do I Relax?

A Piece Of The Past

I Believe Self-Care Is:

Is It Hard For Me To Fall Asleep?

Would I Rather Stay Asleep Than To Wake Up?

Based On My Response To The Previous Prompt, Why Do I Feel This Way?

Do I Have A Hard Time Focusing?

A Piece Of The Past

Do I Feel Love, Happiness And/Or Peace In Any Other Areas Of My Life?

If I Responded Yes To The Previous Prompt, How Long Have I Allowed Myself To Feel Love, Happiness And/Or Peace And What Is This Feeling Towards?

I Have Been Feeling Like:

Based On My Response To The Previous Prompt, How Long Have I Been Feeling This Way?

Have I Sought Out Professional Help?

A Piece Of The Past

If I Answered Yes To The Previous Prompt, What Was The Result?

If I Answered No To The Last Prompt On The Previous Page, Why Not?

Who Do I Feel Like I Can Talk To?

Do I Believe My Feelings Are Normal?

Other People I Know Who Have Shared Similar Traumatic Experiences:

A Piece Of The Past

Do I Have The Support Of My Family And/Or Friends?

How Would I Describe My Current Living Environment?

How Do I Imagine My Life To Be In The Next Five Years?

Are My Religious/Spiritual Beliefs Helping Me?

If I Responded Yes To The Previous Prompt, How Are My Religious/Spiritual Beliefs Helping Me?

A Piece Of The Past

Am I Currently Taking Any Medication/s?

If I Responded Yes To The Previous Prompt, What Medication/s Am I Taking?

When Do I Feel That Certain Traumatic Events Are Happening All Over Again?

What Parts Of My Traumatic Events Can I Not Remember?

What Is Hard For Me To Do?

A Piece Of The Past

What Is Easy For Me To Do?

Am I Easily Irritated?

What Are Some Childhood Traumas That I Have Experienced?

What Do I Believe I Am Over With?

How Have I Been Taught To Cope With Trauma?

A Piece Of The Past

How Do People In My Family Cope With Trauma?

What Have I Silenced Within Me?

It Is Easier For Me To:

How Do I Try To Avoid Reliving The Trauma?

Reliving Traumatic Events:

A Piece Of The Past

What I Wish I Would Have Done Differently In My Traumatic Event?

I Am Tired Of Feeling:

Moving Forward Means:

Leaving It Behind Means:

Around The Holidays, I Feel:

A Piece Of The Past

I Have Done Better With:

A Person Who Has Helped Me To Cope:

Things I Wish I Never Saw:

Who Have I Hurt?

What Have People Close To Me Tried To Get Me To Do?

A Piece Of The Past

What Have I Refused?

Why Have I Refused What Was Mentioned In My Previous Answer?

I Feel Like I Have Control:

What Have Other People Advised Me To Do?

Based On My Previous Response, Why Have They Advised Me To Do This?

A Piece Of The Past

I Feel Safe:

I Am Comfortable:

I Am Capable:

I Am Careful To:

Being 'Me' Again Would Mean:

A Piece Of The Past

I Am Trying To Get Away From:

No One Understands:

I Am Just Trying To Find A Way To:

I Gave Up On:

What I Have Never Told Anyone:

A Piece Of The Past

If Things Were Different:

My Ideal Scenerio:

Because It Is
Getting Better

Because It Is Getting Better

Date: Mood:

Today I Felt: Today I Needed:

Today I Was Triggered By (Answer If   Tommorow I Will Challenge Myself:
Applicable):

Who And/Or What Triggered Me   What Do I Forgive About The Past?
(Answer If Applicable)?

How Did I Respond To My Tigger Today   By Forgiving I Am:
(Answer If Applicable)?

How Did I Make My Trigger Powerless   Today I Stopped/Started/Maintained:
Today?

How Was I Present Today?   How Can I Retell The Story Of A Past
                                               Traumatic Event?

What Thoughts Did I Dwell On That I   I Let Go In Trying To Find The Answer/
Needed To Stop Thinking About That   Reason To:
Caused Unwanted Feelings?

Today I Realized: Tonight's Thoughts:

Because It Is Getting Better

Date: Mood:

Today I Felt: Today I Needed:

Today I Was Triggered By (Answer If   Tommorow I Will Challenge Myself:
Applicable):

Who And/Or What Triggered Me   What Do I Forgive About The Past?
(Answer If Applicable)?

How Did I Respond To My Tigger Today   By Forgiving I Am:
(Answer If Applicable)?

How Did I Make My Trigger Powerless   Today I Stopped/Started/Maintained:
Today?

How Was I Present Today?   How Can I Retell The Story Of A Past
                                             Traumatic Event?

What Thoughts Did I Dwell On That I   I Let Go In Trying To Find The Answer/
Needed To Stop Thinking About That   Reason To:
Caused Unwanted Feelings?

Today I Realized: Tonight's Thoughts:

I Will Heal From This.

Because It Is Getting Better

Date: Mood:

Today I Felt: Today I Needed:

Today I Was Triggered By (Answer If   Tommorow I Will Challenge Myself:
Applicable):

Who And/Or What Triggered Me   What Do I Forgive About The Past?
(Answer If Applicable)?

How Did I Respond To My Tigger Today   By Forgiving I Am:
(Answer If Applicable)?

How Did I Make My Trigger Powerless   Today I Stopped/Started/Maintained:
Today?

How Was I Present Today?   How Can I Retell The Story Of A Past
                                                        Traumatic Event?

What Thoughts Did I Dwell On That I   I Let Go In Trying To Find The Answer/
Needed To Stop Thinking About That   Reason To:
Caused Unwanted Feelings?

Today I Realized: Tonight's Thoughts:

Because It Is Getting Better

Date: Mood:

Today I Felt: Today I Needed:

Today I Was Triggered By (Answer If   Tommorow I Will Challenge Myself:
Applicable):

Who And/Or What Triggered Me   What Do I Forgive About The Past?
(Answer If Applicable)?

How Did I Respond To My Tigger Today   By Forgiving I Am:
(Answer If Applicable)?

How Did I Make My Trigger Powerless   Today I Stopped/Started/Maintained:
Today?

How Was I Present Today?   How Can I Retell The Story Of A Past
                                               Traumatic Event?

What Thoughts Did I Dwell On That I   I Let Go In Trying To Find The Answer/
Needed To Stop Thinking About That   Reason To:
Caused Unwanted Feelings?

Today I Realized: Tonight's Thoughts:

Healing From A Traumatic Experience Feels Like....

Because It Is Getting Better

Date: Mood:

Today I Felt: Today I Needed:

Today I Was Triggered By (Answer If   Tommorow I Will Challenge Myself:
Applicable):

Who And/Or What Triggered Me   What Do I Forgive About The Past?
(Answer If Applicable)?

How Did I Respond To My Tigger Today   By Forgiving I Am:
(Answer If Applicable)?

How Did I Make My Trigger Powerless   Today I Stopped/Started/Maintained:
Today?

How Was I Present Today?   How Can I Retell The Story Of A Past
                                               Traumatic Event?

What Thoughts Did I Dwell On That I   I Let Go In Trying To Find The Answer/
Needed To Stop Thinking About That   Reason To:
Caused Unwanted Feelings?

Today I Realized: Tonight's Thoughts:

I May Never Forget It, But I Will Grow From It.

Because It Is Getting Better

Date: Mood:

Today I Felt: Today I Needed:

Today I Was Triggered By (Answer If   Tommorow I Will Challenge Myself:
Applicable):

Who And/Or What Triggered Me   What Do I Forgive About The Past?
(Answer If Applicable)?

How Did I Respond To My Tigger Today   By Forgiving I Am:
(Answer If Applicable)?

How Did I Make My Trigger Powerless   Today I Stopped/Started/Maintained:
Today?

How Was I Present Today?   How Can I Retell The Story Of A Past
                                               Traumatic Event?

What Thoughts Did I Dwell On That I   I Let Go In Trying To Find The Answer/
Needed To Stop Thinking About That   Reason To:
Caused Unwanted Feelings?

Today I Realized: Tonight's Thoughts:

Life Can Feel So Good If I Choose To Let It.

My Personal Thoughts

Because It Is Getting Better

Date: Mood:

Today I Felt: Today I Needed:

Today I Was Triggered By (Answer If   Tommorow I Will Challenge Myself:
Applicable):

Who And/Or What Triggered Me   What Do I Forgive About The Past?
(Answer If Applicable)?

How Did I Respond To My Tigger Today   By Forgiving I Am:
(Answer If Applicable)?

How Did I Make My Trigger Powerless   Today I Stopped/Started/Maintained:
Today?

How Was I Present Today?   How Can I Retell The Story Of A Past
                                         Traumatic Event?

What Thoughts Did I Dwell On That I   I Let Go In Trying To Find The Answer/
Needed To Stop Thinking About That   Reason To:
Caused Unwanted Feelings?

Today I Realized: Tonight's Thoughts:

Because It Is Getting Better

Date: Mood:

Today I Felt: Today I Needed:

Today I Was Triggered By (Answer If   Tommorow I Will Challenge Myself:
Applicable):

Who And/Or What Triggered Me   What Do I Forgive About The Past?
(Answer If Applicable)?

How Did I Respond To My Tigger Today   By Forgiving I Am:
(Answer If Applicable)?

How Did I Make My Trigger Powerless   Today I Stopped/Started/Maintained:
Today?

How Was I Present Today?   How Can I Retell The Story Of A Past
                                               Traumatic Event?

What Thoughts Did I Dwell On That I   I Let Go In Trying To Find The Answer/
Needed To Stop Thinking About That   Reason To:
Caused Unwanted Feelings?

Today I Realized: Tonight's Thoughts:

Because It Is Getting Better

Date: Mood:

Today I Felt: Today I Needed:

Today I Was Triggered By (Answer If   Tommorow I Will Challenge Myself:
Applicable):

Who And/Or What Triggered Me   What Do I Forgive About The Past?
(Answer If Applicable)?

How Did I Respond To My Tigger Today   By Forgiving I Am:
(Answer If Applicable)?

How Did I Make My Trigger Powerless   Today I Stopped/Started/Maintained:
Today?

How Was I Present Today?   How Can I Retell The Story Of A Past
                                               Traumatic Event?

What Thoughts Did I Dwell On That I   I Let Go In Trying To Find The Answer/
Needed To Stop Thinking About That   Reason To:
Caused Unwanted Feelings?

Today I Realized: Tonight's Thoughts:

I Am What I Choose To Become.

I Am Gentle With Me.

Because It Is Getting Better

Date: | Mood:

Today I Felt: | Today I Needed:

Today I Was Triggered By (Answer If Applicable): | Tommorow I Will Challenge Myself:

Who And/Or What Triggered Me (Answer If Applicable)? | What Do I Forgive About The Past?

How Did I Respond To My Tigger Today (Answer If Applicable)? | By Forgiving I Am:

How Did I Make My Trigger Powerless Today? | Today I Stopped/Started/Maintained:

How Was I Present Today? | How Can I Retell The Story Of A Past Traumatic Event?

What Thoughts Did I Dwell On That I Needed To Stop Thinking About That Caused Unwanted Feelings? | I Let Go In Trying To Find The Answer/ Reason To:

Today I Realized: | Tonight's Thoughts:

Because It Is Getting Better

Date: Mood:

Today I Felt: Today I Needed:

Today I Was Triggered By (Answer If   Tommorow I Will Challenge Myself:
Applicable):

Who And/Or What Triggered Me   What Do I Forgive About The Past?
(Answer If Applicable)?

How Did I Respond To My Tigger Today   By Forgiving I Am:
(Answer If Applicable)?

How Did I Make My Trigger Powerless   Today I Stopped/Started/Maintained:
Today?

How Was I Present Today?   How Can I Retell The Story Of A Past
                                               Traumatic Event?

What Thoughts Did I Dwell On That I   I Let Go In Trying To Find The Answer/
Needed To Stop Thinking About That   Reason To:
Caused Unwanted Feelings?

Today I Realized: Tonight's Thoughts:

Because It Is Getting Better

Date: Mood:

Today I Felt: Today I Needed:

Today I Was Triggered By (Answer If   Tommorow I Will Challenge Myself:
Applicable):

Who And/Or What Triggered Me   What Do I Forgive About The Past?
(Answer If Applicable)?

How Did I Respond To My Tigger Today   By Forgiving I Am:
(Answer If Applicable)?

How Did I Make My Trigger Powerless   Today I Stopped/Started/Maintained:
Today?

How Was I Present Today?   How Can I Retell The Story Of A Past
                                               Traumatic Event?

What Thoughts Did I Dwell On That I   I Let Go In Trying To Find The Answer/
Needed To Stop Thinking About That   Reason To:
Caused Unwanted Feelings?

Today I Realized: Tonight's Thoughts:

Promises I Am Making To Myself....

I Deserve A Good Life.

Because It Is Getting Better

Date: Mood:

Today I Felt: Today I Needed:

Today I Was Triggered By (Answer If   Tommorow I Will Challenge Myself:
Applicable):

Who And/Or What Triggered Me   What Do I Forgive About The Past?
(Answer If Applicable)?

How Did I Respond To My Tigger Today   By Forgiving I Am:
(Answer If Applicable)?

How Did I Make My Trigger Powerless   Today I Stopped/Started/Maintained:
Today?

How Was I Present Today?   How Can I Retell The Story Of A Past
                                                Traumatic Event?

What Thoughts Did I Dwell On That I   I Let Go In Trying To Find The Answer/
Needed To Stop Thinking About That   Reason To:
Caused Unwanted Feelings?

Today I Realized: Tonight's Thoughts:

Because It Is Getting Better

Date: Mood:

Today I Felt: Today I Needed:

Today I Was Triggered By (Answer If   Tommorow I Will Challenge Myself:
Applicable):

Who And/Or What Triggered Me   What Do I Forgive About The Past?
(Answer If Applicable)?

How Did I Respond To My Tigger Today   By Forgiving I Am:
(Answer If Applicable)?

How Did I Make My Trigger Powerless   Today I Stopped/Started/Maintained:
Today?

How Was I Present Today?   How Can I Retell The Story Of A Past
                                               Traumatic Event?

What Thoughts Did I Dwell On That I   I Let Go In Trying To Find The Answer/
Needed To Stop Thinking About That   Reason To:
Caused Unwanted Feelings?

Today I Realized: Tonight's Thoughts:

My Personal Thoughts

Because It Is Getting Better

Date: Mood:

Today I Felt: Today I Needed:

Today I Was Triggered By (Answer If   Tommorow I Will Challenge Myself:
Applicable):

Who And/Or What Triggered Me   What Do I Forgive About The Past?
(Answer If Applicable)?

How Did I Respond To My Tigger Today   By Forgiving I Am:
(Answer If Applicable)?

How Did I Make My Trigger Powerless   Today I Stopped/Started/Maintained:
Today?

How Was I Present Today?   How Can I Retell The Story Of A Past
                                         Traumatic Event?

What Thoughts Did I Dwell On That I   I Let Go In Trying To Find The Answer/
Needed To Stop Thinking About That   Reason To:
Caused Unwanted Feelings?

Today I Realized: Tonight's Thoughts:

Because It Is Getting Better

Date: Mood:

Today I Felt: Today I Needed:

Today I Was Triggered By (Answer If   Tommorow I Will Challenge Myself:
Applicable):

Who And/Or What Triggered Me   What Do I Forgive About The Past?
(Answer If Applicable)?

How Did I Respond To My Tigger Today   By Forgiving I Am:
(Answer If Applicable)?

How Did I Make My Trigger Powerless   Today I Stopped/Started/Maintained:
Today?

How Was I Present Today?   How Can I Retell The Story Of A Past
                                                   Traumatic Event?

What Thoughts Did I Dwell On That I   I Let Go In Trying To Find The Answer/
Needed To Stop Thinking About That   Reason To:
Caused Unwanted Feelings?

Today I Realized: Tonight's Thoughts:

I Am Forgiven.

It Is Not My Fault.

Because It Is Getting Better

Date: Mood:

Today I Felt: Today I Needed:

Today I Was Triggered By (Answer If   Tommorow I Will Challenge Myself:
Applicable):

Who And/Or What Triggered Me   What Do I Forgive About The Past?
(Answer If Applicable)?

How Did I Respond To My Tigger Today   By Forgiving I Am:
(Answer If Applicable)?

How Did I Make My Trigger Powerless   Today I Stopped/Started/Maintained:
Today?

How Was I Present Today?   How Can I Retell The Story Of A Past
                                         Traumatic Event?

What Thoughts Did I Dwell On That I   I Let Go In Trying To Find The Answer/
Needed To Stop Thinking About That   Reason To:
Caused Unwanted Feelings?

Today I Realized: Tonight's Thoughts:

Because It Is Getting Better

Date: Mood:

Today I Felt: Today I Needed:

Today I Was Triggered By (Answer If   Tommorow I Will Challenge Myself:
Applicable):

Who And/Or What Triggered Me   What Do I Forgive About The Past?
(Answer If Applicable)?

How Did I Respond To My Tigger Today   By Forgiving I Am:
(Answer If Applicable)?

How Did I Make My Trigger Powerless   Today I Stopped/Started/Maintained:
Today?

How Was I Present Today?   How Can I Retell The Story Of A Past
                                               Traumatic Event?

What Thoughts Did I Dwell On That I   I Let Go In Trying To Find The Answer/
Needed To Stop Thinking About That   Reason To:
Caused Unwanted Feelings?

Today I Realized: Tonight's Thoughts:

My Five Life Goals....

1.

2.

3.

4.

5.

Because It Is Getting Better

Date: Mood:

Today I Felt: Today I Needed:

Today I Was Triggered By (Answer If   Tommorow I Will Challenge Myself:
Applicable):

Who And/Or What Triggered Me   What Do I Forgive About The Past?
(Answer If Applicable)?

How Did I Respond To My Tigger Today   By Forgiving I Am:
(Answer If Applicable)?

How Did I Make My Trigger Powerless   Today I Stopped/Started/Maintained:
Today?

How Was I Present Today?   How Can I Retell The Story Of A Past
                                               Traumatic Event?

What Thoughts Did I Dwell On That I   I Let Go In Trying To Find The Answer/
Needed To Stop Thinking About That   Reason To:
Caused Unwanted Feelings?

Today I Realized: Tonight's Thoughts:

Because It Is Getting Better

Date: Mood:

Today I Felt: Today I Needed:

Today I Was Triggered By (Answer If   Tommorow I Will Challenge Myself:
Applicable):

Who And/Or What Triggered Me   What Do I Forgive About The Past?
(Answer If Applicable)?

How Did I Respond To My Tigger Today   By Forgiving I Am:
(Answer If Applicable)?

How Did I Make My Trigger Powerless   Today I Stopped/Started/Maintained:
Today?

How Was I Present Today?   How Can I Retell The Story Of A Past
                                         Traumatic Event?

What Thoughts Did I Dwell On That I   I Let Go In Trying To Find The Answer/
Needed To Stop Thinking About That   Reason To:
Caused Unwanted Feelings?

Today I Realized: Tonight's Thoughts:

Because It Is Getting Better

Date: Mood:

Today I Felt: Today I Needed:

Today I Was Triggered By (Answer If   Tommorow I Will Challenge Myself:
Applicable):

Who And/Or What Triggered Me   What Do I Forgive About The Past?
(Answer If Applicable)?

How Did I Respond To My Tigger Today   By Forgiving I Am:
(Answer If Applicable)?

How Did I Make My Trigger Powerless   Today I Stopped/Started/Maintained:
Today?

How Was I Present Today?   How Can I Retell The Story Of A Past
                                               Traumatic Event?

What Thoughts Did I Dwell On That I   I Let Go In Trying To Find The Answer/
Needed To Stop Thinking About That   Reason To:
Caused Unwanted Feelings?

Today I Realized: Tonight's Thoughts:

86

Because It Is Getting Better

Date: Mood:

Today I Felt: Today I Needed:

Today I Was Triggered By (Answer If   Tommorow I Will Challenge Myself:
Applicable):

Who And/Or What Triggered Me   What Do I Forgive About The Past?
(Answer If Applicable)?

How Did I Respond To My Tigger Today   By Forgiving I Am:
(Answer If Applicable)?

How Did I Make My Trigger Powerless   Today I Stopped/Started/Maintained:
Today?

How Was I Present Today?   How Can I Retell The Story Of A Past
                                                Traumatic Event?

What Thoughts Did I Dwell On That I   I Let Go In Trying To Find The Answer/
Needed To Stop Thinking About That   Reason To:
Caused Unwanted Feelings?

Today I Realized: Tonight's Thoughts:

My Personal Thoughts

No Longer Am I Allowing Other People To Remind Me Of My Past When I Have A Bright Future Ahead.

Because It Is Getting Better

Date: Mood:

Today I Felt: Today I Needed:

Today I Was Triggered By (Answer If   Tommorow I Will Challenge Myself:
Applicable):

Who And/Or What Triggered Me   What Do I Forgive About The Past?
(Answer If Applicable)?

How Did I Respond To My Tigger Today   By Forgiving I Am:
(Answer If Applicable)?

How Did I Make My Trigger Powerless   Today I Stopped/Started/Maintained:
Today?

How Was I Present Today?   How Can I Retell The Story Of A Past
                                                Traumatic Event?

What Thoughts Did I Dwell On That I   I Let Go In Trying To Find The Answer/
Needed To Stop Thinking About That   Reason To:
Caused Unwanted Feelings?

Today I Realized: Tonight's Thoughts:

Because It Is Getting Better

Date: Mood:

Today I Felt: Today I Needed:

Today I Was Triggered By (Answer If   Tommorow I Will Challenge Myself:
Applicable):

Who And/Or What Triggered Me   What Do I Forgive About The Past?
(Answer If Applicable)?

How Did I Respond To My Tigger Today   By Forgiving I Am:
(Answer If Applicable)?

How Did I Make My Trigger Powerless   Today I Stopped/Started/Maintained:
Today?

How Was I Present Today?   How Can I Retell The Story Of A Past
                                               Traumatic Event?

What Thoughts Did I Dwell On That I   I Let Go In Trying To Find The Answer/
Needed To Stop Thinking About That   Reason To:
Caused Unwanted Feelings?

Today I Realized: Tonight's Thoughts:

Because It Is Getting Better

Date: Mood:

Today I Felt: Today I Needed:

Today I Was Triggered By (Answer If   Tommorow I Will Challenge Myself:
Applicable):

Who And/Or What Triggered Me   What Do I Forgive About The Past?
(Answer If Applicable)?

How Did I Respond To My Tigger Today   By Forgiving I Am:
(Answer If Applicable)?

How Did I Make My Trigger Powerless   Today I Stopped/Started/Maintained:
Today?

How Was I Present Today?   How Can I Retell The Story Of A Past
                                               Traumatic Event?

What Thoughts Did I Dwell On That I   I Let Go In Trying To Find The Answer/
Needed To Stop Thinking About That   Reason To:
Caused Unwanted Feelings?

Today I Realized: Tonight's Thoughts:

I Overcame The Unexpected.

What Happened To Me Does Not Dictate Where I Am Going.

Because It Is Getting Better

Date: Mood:

Today I Felt: Today I Needed:

Today I Was Triggered By (Answer If   Tommorow I Will Challenge Myself:
Applicable):

Who And/Or What Triggered Me   What Do I Forgive About The Past?
(Answer If Applicable)?

How Did I Respond To My Tigger Today   By Forgiving I Am:
(Answer If Applicable)?

How Did I Make My Trigger Powerless   Today I Stopped/Started/Maintained:
Today?

How Was I Present Today?   How Can I Retell The Story Of A Past
                                               Traumatic Event?

What Thoughts Did I Dwell On That I   I Let Go In Trying To Find The Answer/
Needed To Stop Thinking About That   Reason To:
Caused Unwanted Feelings?

Today I Realized: Tonight's Thoughts:

Because It Is Getting Better

Date: Mood:

Today I Felt: Today I Needed:

Today I Was Triggered By (Answer If   Tommorow I Will Challenge Myself:
Applicable):

Who And/Or What Triggered Me   What Do I Forgive About The Past?
(Answer If Applicable)?

How Did I Respond To My Tigger Today   By Forgiving I Am:
(Answer If Applicable)?

How Did I Make My Trigger Powerless   Today I Stopped/Started/Maintained:
Today?

How Was I Present Today?   How Can I Retell The Story Of A Past
                                         Traumatic Event?

What Thoughts Did I Dwell On That I   I Let Go In Trying To Find The Answer/
Needed To Stop Thinking About That   Reason To:
Caused Unwanted Feelings?

Today I Realized: Tonight's Thoughts:

What I Refuse To Miss Out On....

Because It Is Getting Better

Date: Mood:

Today I Felt: Today I Needed:

Today I Was Triggered By (Answer If   Tommorow I Will Challenge Myself:
Applicable):

Who And/Or What Triggered Me   What Do I Forgive About The Past?
(Answer If Applicable)?

How Did I Respond To My Tigger Today   By Forgiving I Am:
(Answer If Applicable)?

How Did I Make My Trigger Powerless   Today I Stopped/Started/Maintained:
Today?

How Was I Present Today?   How Can I Retell The Story Of A Past
                                               Traumatic Event?

What Thoughts Did I Dwell On That I   I Let Go In Trying To Find The Answer/
Needed To Stop Thinking About That   Reason To:
Caused Unwanted Feelings?

Today I Realized: Tonight's Thoughts:

Because It Is Getting Better

Date: Mood:

Today I Felt: Today I Needed:

Today I Was Triggered By (Answer If   Tommorow I Will Challenge Myself:
Applicable):

Who And/Or What Triggered Me   What Do I Forgive About The Past?
(Answer If Applicable)?

How Did I Respond To My Tigger Today   By Forgiving I Am:
(Answer If Applicable)?

How Did I Make My Trigger Powerless   Today I Stopped/Started/Maintained:
Today?

How Was I Present Today?   How Can I Retell The Story Of A Past
                                               Traumatic Event?

What Thoughts Did I Dwell On That I   I Let Go In Trying To Find The Answer/
Needed To Stop Thinking About That   Reason To:
Caused Unwanted Feelings?

Today I Realized: Tonight's Thoughts:

My Personal Thoughts

Because It Is Getting Better

Date: Mood:

Today I Felt: Today I Needed:

Today I Was Triggered By (Answer If   Tommorow I Will Challenge Myself:
Applicable):

Who And/Or What Triggered Me   What Do I Forgive About The Past?
(Answer If Applicable)?

How Did I Respond To My Tigger Today   By Forgiving I Am:
(Answer If Applicable)?

How Did I Make My Trigger Powerless   Today I Stopped/Started/Maintained:
Today?

How Was I Present Today?   How Can I Retell The Story Of A Past
                                               Traumatic Event?

What Thoughts Did I Dwell On That I   I Let Go In Trying To Find The Answer/
Needed To Stop Thinking About That   Reason To:
Caused Unwanted Feelings?

Today I Realized: Tonight's Thoughts:

Because It Is Getting Better

Date: Mood:

Today I Felt: Today I Needed:

Today I Was Triggered By (Answer If   Tommorow I Will Challenge Myself:
Applicable):

Who And/Or What Triggered Me   What Do I Forgive About The Past?
(Answer If Applicable)?

How Did I Respond To My Tigger Today   By Forgiving I Am:
(Answer If Applicable)?

How Did I Make My Trigger Powerless   Today I Stopped/Started/Maintained:
Today?

How Was I Present Today?   How Can I Retell The Story Of A Past
                                               Traumatic Event?

What Thoughts Did I Dwell On That I   I Let Go In Trying To Find The Answer/
Needed To Stop Thinking About That   Reason To:
Caused Unwanted Feelings?

Today I Realized: Tonight's Thoughts:

I Forgive Those That Have Hurt Me.

Because It Is Getting Better

Date: Mood:

Today I Felt: Today I Needed:

Today I Was Triggered By (Answer If   Tommorow I Will Challenge Myself:
Applicable):

Who And/Or What Triggered Me   What Do I Forgive About The Past?
(Answer If Applicable)?

How Did I Respond To My Tigger Today   By Forgiving I Am:
(Answer If Applicable)?

How Did I Make My Trigger Powerless   Today I Stopped/Started/Maintained:
Today?

How Was I Present Today?   How Can I Retell The Story Of A Past
                                               Traumatic Event?

What Thoughts Did I Dwell On That I   I Let Go In Trying To Find The Answer/
Needed To Stop Thinking About That   Reason To:
Caused Unwanted Feelings?

Today I Realized: Tonight's Thoughts:

Because It Is Getting Better

Date: Mood:

Today I Felt: Today I Needed:

Today I Was Triggered By (Answer If   Tommorow I Will Challenge Myself:
Applicable):

Who And/Or What Triggered Me   What Do I Forgive About The Past?
(Answer If Applicable)?

How Did I Respond To My Tigger Today   By Forgiving I Am:
(Answer If Applicable)?

How Did I Make My Trigger Powerless   Today I Stopped/Started/Maintained:
Today?

How Was I Present Today?   How Can I Retell The Story Of A Past
                                               Traumatic Event?

What Thoughts Did I Dwell On That I   I Let Go In Trying To Find The Answer/
Needed To Stop Thinking About That   Reason To:
Caused Unwanted Feelings?

Today I Realized: Tonight's Thoughts:

Seven Ways For Me To Be Present....

1.

2.

3.

4.

5.

6.

7.

Because It Is Getting Better

Date: Mood:

Today I Felt: Today I Needed:

Today I Was Triggered By (Answer If   Tommorow I Will Challenge Myself:
Applicable):

Who And/Or What Triggered Me   What Do I Forgive About The Past?
(Answer If Applicable)?

How Did I Respond To My Tigger Today   By Forgiving I Am:
(Answer If Applicable)?

How Did I Make My Trigger Powerless   Today I Stopped/Started/Maintained:
Today?

How Was I Present Today?   How Can I Retell The Story Of A Past
                                                   Traumatic Event?

What Thoughts Did I Dwell On That I   I Let Go In Trying To Find The Answer/
Needed To Stop Thinking About That   Reason To:
Caused Unwanted Feelings?

Today I Realized: Tonight's Thoughts:

Because It Is Getting Better

Date: Mood:

Today I Felt: Today I Needed:

Today I Was Triggered By (Answer If   Tommorow I Will Challenge Myself:
Applicable):

Who And/Or What Triggered Me   What Do I Forgive About The Past?
(Answer If Applicable)?

How Did I Respond To My Tigger Today   By Forgiving I Am:
(Answer If Applicable)?

How Did I Make My Trigger Powerless   Today I Stopped/Started/Maintained:
Today?

How Was I Present Today?   How Can I Retell The Story Of A Past
                                         Traumatic Event?

What Thoughts Did I Dwell On That I   I Let Go In Trying To Find The Answer/
Needed To Stop Thinking About That   Reason To:
Caused Unwanted Feelings?

Today I Realized: Tonight's Thoughts:

Because It Is Getting Better

Date: Mood:

Today I Felt: Today I Needed:

Today I Was Triggered By (Answer If   Tommorow I Will Challenge Myself:
Applicable):

Who And/Or What Triggered Me   What Do I Forgive About The Past?
(Answer If Applicable)?

How Did I Respond To My Tigger Today   By Forgiving I Am:
(Answer If Applicable)?

How Did I Make My Trigger Powerless   Today I Stopped/Started/Maintained:
Today?

How Was I Present Today?   How Can I Retell The Story Of A Past
                                               Traumatic Event?

What Thoughts Did I Dwell On That I   I Let Go In Trying To Find The Answer/
Needed To Stop Thinking About That   Reason To:
Caused Unwanted Feelings?

Today I Realized: Tonight's Thoughts:

My Personal Thoughts

Because It Is Getting Better

Date: Mood:

Today I Felt: Today I Needed:

Today I Was Triggered By (Answer If   Tommorow I Will Challenge Myself:
Applicable):

Who And/Or What Triggered Me   What Do I Forgive About The Past?
(Answer If Applicable)?

How Did I Respond To My Tigger Today   By Forgiving I Am:
(Answer If Applicable)?

How Did I Make My Trigger Powerless   Today I Stopped/Started/Maintained:
Today?

How Was I Present Today?   How Can I Retell The Story Of A Past
                                         Traumatic Event?

What Thoughts Did I Dwell On That I   I Let Go In Trying To Find The Answer/
Needed To Stop Thinking About That   Reason To:
Caused Unwanted Feelings?

Today I Realized: Tonight's Thoughts:

I Stopped Asking Why.

I Am Mindful Of....

Because It Is Getting Better

Date: Mood:

Today I Felt: Today I Needed:

Today I Was Triggered By (Answer If   Tommorow I Will Challenge Myself:
Applicable):

Who And/Or What Triggered Me   What Do I Forgive About The Past?
(Answer If Applicable)?

How Did I Respond To My Tigger Today   By Forgiving I Am:
(Answer If Applicable)?

How Did I Make My Trigger Powerless   Today I Stopped/Started/Maintained:
Today?

How Was I Present Today?   How Can I Retell The Story Of A Past
                                               Traumatic Event?

What Thoughts Did I Dwell On That I   I Let Go In Trying To Find The Answer/
Needed To Stop Thinking About That   Reason To:
Caused Unwanted Feelings?

Today I Realized: Tonight's Thoughts:

Because It Is Getting Better

Date: Mood:

Today I Felt: Today I Needed:

Today I Was Triggered By (Answer If   Tommorow I Will Challenge Myself:
Applicable):

Who And/Or What Triggered Me   What Do I Forgive About The Past?
(Answer If Applicable)?

How Did I Respond To My Tigger Today   By Forgiving I Am:
(Answer If Applicable)?

How Did I Make My Trigger Powerless   Today I Stopped/Started/Maintained:
Today?

How Was I Present Today?   How Can I Retell The Story Of A Past
                                               Traumatic Event?

What Thoughts Did I Dwell On That I   I Let Go In Trying To Find The Answer/
Needed To Stop Thinking About That   Reason To:
Caused Unwanted Feelings?

Today I Realized: Tonight's Thoughts:

Because It Is Getting Better

Date: Mood:

Today I Felt: Today I Needed:

Today I Was Triggered By (Answer If   Tommorow I Will Challenge Myself:
Applicable):

Who And/Or What Triggered Me   What Do I Forgive About The Past?
(Answer If Applicable)?

How Did I Respond To My Tigger Today   By Forgiving I Am:
(Answer If Applicable)?

How Did I Make My Trigger Powerless   Today I Stopped/Started/Maintained:
Today?

How Was I Present Today?   How Can I Retell The Story Of A Past
                                               Traumatic Event?

What Thoughts Did I Dwell On That I   I Let Go In Trying To Find The Answer/
Needed To Stop Thinking About That   Reason To:
Caused Unwanted Feelings?

Today I Realized: Tonight's Thoughts:

Because It Is Getting Better

Date: Mood:

Today I Felt: Today I Needed:

Today I Was Triggered By (Answer If   Tommorow I Will Challenge Myself:
Applicable):

Who And/Or What Triggered Me   What Do I Forgive About The Past?
(Answer If Applicable)?

How Did I Respond To My Tigger Today   By Forgiving I Am:
(Answer If Applicable)?

How Did I Make My Trigger Powerless   Today I Stopped/Started/Maintained:
Today?

How Was I Present Today?   How Can I Retell The Story Of A Past
                                               Traumatic Event?

What Thoughts Did I Dwell On That I   I Let Go In Trying To Find The Answer/
Needed To Stop Thinking About That   Reason To:
Caused Unwanted Feelings?

Today I Realized: Tonight's Thoughts:

My Personal Thoughts

I Am Allowing Those Who Want To Love Me Access To Love Me In The Healthiest Way.

Because It Is Getting Better

Date: Mood:

Today I Felt: Today I Needed:

Today I Was Triggered By (Answer If   Tommorow I Will Challenge Myself:
Applicable):

Who And/Or What Triggered Me   What Do I Forgive About The Past?
(Answer If Applicable)?

How Did I Respond To My Tigger Today   By Forgiving I Am:
(Answer If Applicable)?

How Did I Make My Trigger Powerless   Today I Stopped/Started/Maintained:
Today?

How Was I Present Today?   How Can I Retell The Story Of A Past
                                               Traumatic Event?

What Thoughts Did I Dwell On That I   I Let Go In Trying To Find The Answer/
Needed To Stop Thinking About That   Reason To:
Caused Unwanted Feelings?

Today I Realized: Tonight's Thoughts:

Because It Is Getting Better

Date:

Mood:

Today I Felt:

Today I Needed:

Today I Was Triggered By (Answer If Applicable):

Tommorow I Will Challenge Myself:

Who And/Or What Triggered Me (Answer If Applicable)?

What Do I Forgive About The Past?

How Did I Respond To My Tigger Today (Answer If Applicable)?

By Forgiving I Am:

How Did I Make My Trigger Powerless Today?

Today I Stopped/Started/Maintained:

How Was I Present Today?

How Can I Retell The Story Of A Past Traumatic Event?

What Thoughts Did I Dwell On That I Needed To Stop Thinking About That Caused Unwanted Feelings?

I Let Go In Trying To Find The Answer/ Reason To:

Today I Realized:

Tonight's Thoughts:

It Has Taken Me....

To Learn....

Because It Is Getting Better

Date: Mood:

Today I Felt: Today I Needed:

Today I Was Triggered By (Answer If   Tommorow I Will Challenge Myself:
Applicable):

Who And/Or What Triggered Me   What Do I Forgive About The Past?
(Answer If Applicable)?

How Did I Respond To My Tigger Today   By Forgiving I Am:
(Answer If Applicable)?

How Did I Make My Trigger Powerless   Today I Stopped/Started/Maintained:
Today?

How Was I Present Today?   How Can I Retell The Story Of A Past
                                               Traumatic Event?

What Thoughts Did I Dwell On That I   I Let Go In Trying To Find The Answer/
Needed To Stop Thinking About That   Reason To:
Caused Unwanted Feelings?

Today I Realized: Tonight's Thoughts:

Because It Is Getting Better

Date: Mood:

Today I Felt: Today I Needed:

Today I Was Triggered By (Answer If   Tommorow I Will Challenge Myself:
Applicable):

Who And/Or What Triggered Me   What Do I Forgive About The Past?
(Answer If Applicable)?

How Did I Respond To My Tigger Today   By Forgiving I Am:
(Answer If Applicable)?

How Did I Make My Trigger Powerless   Today I Stopped/Started/Maintained:
Today?

How Was I Present Today?   How Can I Retell The Story Of A Past
                                               Traumatic Event?

What Thoughts Did I Dwell On That I   I Let Go In Trying To Find The Answer/
Needed To Stop Thinking About That   Reason To:
Caused Unwanted Feelings?

Today I Realized: Tonight's Thoughts:

Because It Is Getting Better

Date: Mood:

Today I Felt: Today I Needed:

Today I Was Triggered By (Answer If   Tommorow I Will Challenge Myself:
Applicable):

Who And/Or What Triggered Me   What Do I Forgive About The Past?
(Answer If Applicable)?

How Did I Respond To My Tigger Today   By Forgiving I Am:
(Answer If Applicable)?

How Did I Make My Trigger Powerless   Today I Stopped/Started/Maintained:
Today?

How Was I Present Today?   How Can I Retell The Story Of A Past
                                               Traumatic Event?

What Thoughts Did I Dwell On That I   I Let Go In Trying To Find The Answer/
Needed To Stop Thinking About That   Reason To:
Caused Unwanted Feelings?

Today I Realized: Tonight's Thoughts:

My Personal Thoughts

Because It Is Getting Better

Date: Mood:

Today I Felt: Today I Needed:

Today I Was Triggered By (Answer If   Tommorow I Will Challenge Myself:
Applicable):

Who And/Or What Triggered Me   What Do I Forgive About The Past?
(Answer If Applicable)?

How Did I Respond To My Tigger Today   By Forgiving I Am:
(Answer If Applicable)?

How Did I Make My Trigger Powerless   Today I Stopped/Started/Maintained:
Today?

How Was I Present Today?   How Can I Retell The Story Of A Past
                                             Traumatic Event?

What Thoughts Did I Dwell On That I   I Let Go In Trying To Find The Answer/
Needed To Stop Thinking About That   Reason To:
Caused Unwanted Feelings?

Today I Realized: Tonight's Thoughts:

Because It Is Getting Better

Date: Mood:

Today I Felt: Today I Needed:

Today I Was Triggered By (Answer If   Tommorow I Will Challenge Myself:
Applicable):

Who And/Or What Triggered Me   What Do I Forgive About The Past?
(Answer If Applicable)?

How Did I Respond To My Tigger Today   By Forgiving I Am:
(Answer If Applicable)?

How Did I Make My Trigger Powerless   Today I Stopped/Started/Maintained:
Today?

How Was I Present Today?   How Can I Retell The Story Of A Past
                                         Traumatic Event?

What Thoughts Did I Dwell On That I   I Let Go In Trying To Find The Answer/
Needed To Stop Thinking About That   Reason To:
Caused Unwanted Feelings?

Today I Realized: Tonight's Thoughts:

Because It Is Getting Better

Date: | Mood:

Today I Felt: | Today I Needed:

Today I Was Triggered By (Answer If Applicable): | Tommorow I Will Challenge Myself:

Who And/Or What Triggered Me (Answer If Applicable)? | What Do I Forgive About The Past?

How Did I Respond To My Tigger Today (Answer If Applicable)? | By Forgiving I Am:

How Did I Make My Trigger Powerless Today? | Today I Stopped/Started/Maintained:

How Was I Present Today? | How Can I Retell The Story Of A Past Traumatic Event?

What Thoughts Did I Dwell On That I Needed To Stop Thinking About That Caused Unwanted Feelings? | I Let Go In Trying To Find The Answer/ Reason To:

Today I Realized: | Tonight's Thoughts:

I Am Taking Pride In How Far I Have Come.

It Really Hurts Me....

Because It Is Getting Better

Date: Mood:

Today I Felt: Today I Needed:

Today I Was Triggered By (Answer If   Tommorow I Will Challenge Myself:
Applicable):

Who And/Or What Triggered Me   What Do I Forgive About The Past?
(Answer If Applicable)?

How Did I Respond To My Tigger Today   By Forgiving I Am:
(Answer If Applicable)?

How Did I Make My Trigger Powerless   Today I Stopped/Started/Maintained:
Today?

How Was I Present Today?   How Can I Retell The Story Of A Past
                                               Traumatic Event?

What Thoughts Did I Dwell On That I   I Let Go In Trying To Find The Answer/
Needed To Stop Thinking About That   Reason To:
Caused Unwanted Feelings?

Today I Realized: Tonight's Thoughts:

Because It Is Getting Better

Date: Mood:

Today I Felt: Today I Needed:

Today I Was Triggered By (Answer If   Tommorow I Will Challenge Myself:
Applicable):

Who And/Or What Triggered Me   What Do I Forgive About The Past?
(Answer If Applicable)?

How Did I Respond To My Tigger Today   By Forgiving I Am:
(Answer If Applicable)?

How Did I Make My Trigger Powerless   Today I Stopped/Started/Maintained:
Today?

How Was I Present Today?   How Can I Retell The Story Of A Past
                                         Traumatic Event?

What Thoughts Did I Dwell On That I   I Let Go In Trying To Find The Answer/
Needed To Stop Thinking About That   Reason To:
Caused Unwanted Feelings?

Today I Realized: Tonight's Thoughts:

Because It Is Getting Better

Date: Mood:

Today I Felt: Today I Needed:

Today I Was Triggered By (Answer If   Tommorow I Will Challenge Myself:
Applicable):

Who And/Or What Triggered Me   What Do I Forgive About The Past?
(Answer If Applicable)?

How Did I Respond To My Tigger Today   By Forgiving I Am:
(Answer If Applicable)?

How Did I Make My Trigger Powerless   Today I Stopped/Started/Maintained:
Today?

How Was I Present Today?   How Can I Retell The Story Of A Past
                                               Traumatic Event?

What Thoughts Did I Dwell On That I   I Let Go In Trying To Find The Answer/
Needed To Stop Thinking About That   Reason To:
Caused Unwanted Feelings?

Today I Realized: Tonight's Thoughts:

My Personal Thoughts

Because It Is Getting Better

Date: Mood:

Today I Felt: Today I Needed:

Today I Was Triggered By (Answer If   Tommorow I Will Challenge Myself:
Applicable):

Who And/Or What Triggered Me   What Do I Forgive About The Past?
(Answer If Applicable)?

How Did I Respond To My Tigger Today   By Forgiving I Am:
(Answer If Applicable)?

How Did I Make My Trigger Powerless   Today I Stopped/Started/Maintained:
Today?

How Was I Present Today?   How Can I Retell The Story Of A Past
                                               Traumatic Event?

What Thoughts Did I Dwell On That I   I Let Go In Trying To Find The Answer/
Needed To Stop Thinking About That   Reason To:
Caused Unwanted Feelings?

Today I Realized: Tonight's Thoughts:

Because It Is Getting Better

Date: Mood:

Today I Felt: Today I Needed:

Today I Was Triggered By (Answer If Applicable):   Tommorow I Will Challenge Myself:

Who And/Or What Triggered Me (Answer If Applicable)?   What Do I Forgive About The Past?

How Did I Respond To My Tigger Today (Answer If Applicable)?   By Forgiving I Am:

How Did I Make My Trigger Powerless Today?   Today I Stopped/Started/Maintained:

How Was I Present Today?   How Can I Retell The Story Of A Past Traumatic Event?

What Thoughts Did I Dwell On That I Needed To Stop Thinking About That Caused Unwanted Feelings?   I Let Go In Trying To Find The Answer/ Reason To:

Today I Realized: Tonight's Thoughts:

The Only Thing I Can Control Is My Mind.

Because It Is Getting Better

Date: Mood:

Today I Felt: Today I Needed:

Today I Was Triggered By (Answer If   Tommorow I Will Challenge Myself:
Applicable):

Who And/Or What Triggered Me   What Do I Forgive About The Past?
(Answer If Applicable)?

How Did I Respond To My Tigger Today   By Forgiving I Am:
(Answer If Applicable)?

How Did I Make My Trigger Powerless   Today I Stopped/Started/Maintained:
Today?

How Was I Present Today?   How Can I Retell The Story Of A Past
                                               Traumatic Event?

What Thoughts Did I Dwell On That I   I Let Go In Trying To Find The Answer/
Needed To Stop Thinking About That   Reason To:
Caused Unwanted Feelings?

Today I Realized: Tonight's Thoughts:

Because It Is Getting Better

Date: Mood:

Today I Felt: Today I Needed:

Today I Was Triggered By (Answer If   Tommorow I Will Challenge Myself:
Applicable):

Who And/Or What Triggered Me   What Do I Forgive About The Past?
(Answer If Applicable)?

How Did I Respond To My Tigger Today   By Forgiving I Am:
(Answer If Applicable)?

How Did I Make My Trigger Powerless   Today I Stopped/Started/Maintained:
Today?

How Was I Present Today?   How Can I Retell The Story Of A Past
                                                Traumatic Event?

What Thoughts Did I Dwell On That I   I Let Go In Trying To Find The Answer/
Needed To Stop Thinking About That   Reason To:
Caused Unwanted Feelings?

Today I Realized: Tonight's Thoughts:

Because It Is Getting Better

Date: Mood:

Today I Felt: Today I Needed:

Today I Was Triggered By (Answer If   Tommorow I Will Challenge Myself:
Applicable):

Who And/Or What Triggered Me   What Do I Forgive About The Past?
(Answer If Applicable)?

How Did I Respond To My Tigger Today   By Forgiving I Am:
(Answer If Applicable)?

How Did I Make My Trigger Powerless   Today I Stopped/Started/Maintained:
Today?

How Was I Present Today?   How Can I Retell The Story Of A Past
                                               Traumatic Event?

What Thoughts Did I Dwell On That I   I Let Go In Trying To Find The Answer/
Needed To Stop Thinking About That   Reason To:
Caused Unwanted Feelings?

Today I Realized: Tonight's Thoughts:

What Do I Want?

My Personal Thoughts

Because It Is Getting Better

Date: Mood:

Today I Felt: Today I Needed:

Today I Was Triggered By (Answer If   Tommorow I Will Challenge Myself:
Applicable):

Who And/Or What Triggered Me   What Do I Forgive About The Past?
(Answer If Applicable)?

How Did I Respond To My Tigger Today   By Forgiving I Am:
(Answer If Applicable)?

How Did I Make My Trigger Powerless   Today I Stopped/Started/Maintained:
Today?

How Was I Present Today?   How Can I Retell The Story Of A Past
                                               Traumatic Event?

What Thoughts Did I Dwell On That I   I Let Go In Trying To Find The Answer/
Needed To Stop Thinking About That   Reason To:
Caused Unwanted Feelings?

Today I Realized: Tonight's Thoughts:

Because It Is Getting Better

Date: Mood:

Today I Felt: Today I Needed:

Today I Was Triggered By (Answer If   Tommorow I Will Challenge Myself:
Applicable):

Who And/Or What Triggered Me   What Do I Forgive About The Past?
(Answer If Applicable)?

How Did I Respond To My Tigger Today   By Forgiving I Am:
(Answer If Applicable)?

How Did I Make My Trigger Powerless   Today I Stopped/Started/Maintained:
Today?

How Was I Present Today?   How Can I Retell The Story Of A Past
                                                Traumatic Event?

What Thoughts Did I Dwell On That I   I Let Go In Trying Io Find The Answer/
Needed To Stop Thinking About That   Reason To:
Caused Unwanted Feelings?

Today I Realized: Tonight's Thoughts:

Because It Is Getting Better

Date: Mood:

Today I Felt: Today I Needed:

Today I Was Triggered By (Answer If   Tommorow I Will Challenge Myself:
Applicable):

Who And/Or What Triggered Me   What Do I Forgive About The Past?
(Answer If Applicable)?

How Did I Respond To My Tigger Today   By Forgiving I Am:
(Answer If Applicable)?

How Did I Make My Trigger Powerless   Today I Stopped/Started/Maintained:
Today?

How Was I Present Today?   How Can I Retell The Story Of A Past
                                               Traumatic Event?

What Thoughts Did I Dwell On That I   I Let Go In Trying To Find The Answer/
Needed To Stop Thinking About That   Reason To:
Caused Unwanted Feelings?

Today I Realized: Tonight's Thoughts:

I Will Keep Working And Believing In Myself.

I Am In A Completely Different Space Then I Was Six Months Ago.

Because It Is Getting Better

Date: Mood:

Today I Felt: Today I Needed:

Today I Was Triggered By (Answer If   Tommorow I Will Challenge Myself:
Applicable):

Who And/Or What Triggered Me   What Do I Forgive About The Past?
(Answer If Applicable)?

How Did I Respond To My Tigger Today   By Forgiving I Am:
(Answer If Applicable)?

How Did I Make My Trigger Powerless   Today I Stopped/Started/Maintained:
Today?

How Was I Present Today?   How Can I Retell The Story Of A Past
                                         Traumatic Event?

What Thoughts Did I Dwell On That I   I Let Go In Trying To Find The Answer/
Needed To Stop Thinking About That   Reason To:
Caused Unwanted Feelings?

Today I Realized: Tonight's Thoughts:

Because It Is Getting Better

Date: Mood:

Today I Felt: Today I Needed:

Today I Was Triggered By (Answer If   Tommorow I Will Challenge Myself:
Applicable):

Who And/Or What Triggered Me   What Do I Forgive About The Past?
(Answer If Applicable)?

How Did I Respond To My Tigger Today   By Forgiving I Am:
(Answer If Applicable)?

How Did I Make My Trigger Powerless   Today I Stopped/Started/Maintained:
Today?

How Was I Present Today?   How Can I Retell The Story Of A Past
                                                Traumatic Event?

What Thoughts Did I Dwell On That I   I Let Go In Trying To Find The Answer/
Needed To Stop Thinking About That   Reason To:
Caused Unwanted Feelings?

Today I Realized: Tonight's Thoughts:

Other People's Traumatic Events Make Me Feel....

Self Love Works.

Because It Is Getting Better

Date: Mood:

Today I Felt: Today I Needed:

Today I Was Triggered By (Answer If   Tommorow I Will Challenge Myself:
Applicable):

Who And/Or What Triggered Me   What Do I Forgive About The Past?
(Answer If Applicable)?

How Did I Respond To My Tigger Today   By Forgiving I Am:
(Answer If Applicable)?

How Did I Make My Trigger Powerless   Today I Stopped/Started/Maintained:
Today?

How Was I Present Today?   How Can I Retell The Story Of A Past
                                                   Traumatic Event?

What Thoughts Did I Dwell On That I   I Let Go In Trying Io Find The Answer/
Needed To Stop Thinking About That   Reason To:
Caused Unwanted Feelings?

Today I Realized: Tonight's Thoughts:

Because It Is Getting Better

Date: Mood:

Today I Felt: Today I Needed:

Today I Was Triggered By (Answer If   Tommorow I Will Challenge Myself:
Applicable):

Who And/Or What Triggered Me   What Do I Forgive About The Past?
(Answer If Applicable)?

How Did I Respond To My Tigger Today   By Forgiving I Am:
(Answer If Applicable)?

How Did I Make My Trigger Powerless   Today I Stopped/Started/Maintained:
Today?

How Was I Present Today?   How Can I Retell The Story Of A Past
                                               Traumatic Event?

What Thoughts Did I Dwell On That I   I Let Go In Trying To Find The Answer/
Needed To Stop Thinking About That   Reason To:
Caused Unwanted Feelings?

Today I Realized: Tonight's Thoughts:

I Have The Courage To Tell My Story.

I Want To Be Known For....

Because It Is Getting Better

Date: Mood:

Today I Felt: Today I Needed:

Today I Was Triggered By (Answer If   Tommorow I Will Challenge Myself:
Applicable):

Who And/Or What Triggered Me   What Do I Forgive About The Past?
(Answer If Applicable)?

How Did I Respond To My Tigger Today   By Forgiving I Am:
(Answer If Applicable)?

How Did I Make My Trigger Powerless   Today I Stopped/Started/Maintained:
Today?

How Was I Present Today?   How Can I Retell The Story Of A Past
                                         Traumatic Event?

What Thoughts Did I Dwell On That I   I Let Go In Trying To Find The Answer/
Needed To Stop Thinking About That   Reason To:
Caused Unwanted Feelings?

Today I Realized: Tonight's Thoughts:

Because It Is Getting Better

Date: Mood:

Today I Felt: Today I Needed:

Today I Was Triggered By (Answer If   Tommorow I Will Challenge Myself:
Applicable):

Who And/Or What Triggered Me   What Do I Forgive About The Past?
(Answer If Applicable)?

How Did I Respond To My Tigger Today   By Forgiving I Am:
(Answer If Applicable)?

How Did I Make My Trigger Powerless   Today I Stopped/Started/Maintained:
Today?

How Was I Present Today?   How Can I Retell The Story Of A Past
                                                          Traumatic Event?

What Thoughts Did I Dwell On That I   I Let Go In Trying To Find The Answer/
Needed To Stop Thinking About That   Reason To:
Caused Unwanted Feelings?

Today I Realized: Tonight's Thoughts:

Because It Is Getting Better

Date: Mood:

Today I Felt: Today I Needed:

Today I Was Triggered By (Answer If Applicable):   Tommorow I Will Challenge Myself:

Who And/Or What Triggered Me (Answer If Applicable)?   What Do I Forgive About The Past?

How Did I Respond To My Tigger Today (Answer If Applicable)?   By Forgiving I Am:

How Did I Make My Trigger Powerless Today?   Today I Stopped/Started/Maintained:

How Was I Present Today?   How Can I Retell The Story Of A Past Traumatic Event?

What Thoughts Did I Dwell On That I Needed To Stop Thinking About That Caused Unwanted Feelings?   I Let Go In Trying To Find The Answer/Reason To:

Today I Realized: Tonight's Thoughts:

My Personal Thoughts

I Stopped Ignoring The Issue.

Because It Is Getting Better

Date: Mood:

Today I Felt: Today I Needed:

Today I Was Triggered By (Answer If   Tommorow I Will Challenge Myself:
Applicable):

Who And/Or What Triggered Me   What Do I Forgive About The Past?
(Answer If Applicable)?

How Did I Respond To My Tigger Today   By Forgiving I Am:
(Answer If Applicable)?

How Did I Make My Trigger Powerless   Today I Stopped/Started/Maintained:
Today?

How Was I Present Today?   How Can I Retell The Story Of A Past
                                               Traumatic Event?

What Thoughts Did I Dwell On That I   I Let Go In Trying To Find The Answer/
Needed To Stop Thinking About That   Reason To:
Caused Unwanted Feelings?

Today I Realized: Tonight's Thoughts:

Because It Is Getting Better

Date: Mood:

Today I Felt: Today I Needed:

Today I Was Triggered By (Answer If   Tommorow I Will Challenge Myself:
Applicable):

Who And/Or What Triggered Me   What Do I Forgive About The Past?
(Answer If Applicable)?

How Did I Respond To My Tigger Today   By Forgiving I Am:
(Answer If Applicable)?

How Did I Make My Trigger Powerless   Today I Stopped/Started/Maintained:
Today?

How Was I Present Today?   How Can I Retell The Story Of A Past
                                          Traumatic Event?

What Thoughts Did I Dwell On That I   I Let Go In Trying To Find The Answer/
Needed To Stop Thinking About That   Reason To:
Caused Unwanted Feelings?

Today I Realized: Tonight's Thoughts:

How Do I Help Other People With Their Traumatic Events?

My Personal Thoughts

Because It Is Getting Better

Date: | Mood:

Today I Felt: | Today I Needed:

Today I Was Triggered By (Answer If Applicable): | Tommorow I Will Challenge Myself:

Who And/Or What Triggered Me (Answer If Applicable)? | What Do I Forgive About The Past?

How Did I Respond To My Tigger Today (Answer If Applicable)? | By Forgiving I Am:

How Did I Make My Trigger Powerless Today? | Today I Stopped/Started/Maintained:

How Was I Present Today? | How Can I Retell The Story Of A Past Traumatic Event?

What Thoughts Did I Dwell On That I Needed To Stop Thinking About That Caused Unwanted Feelings? | I Let Go In Trying To Find The Answer/ Reason To:

Today I Realized: | Tonight's Thoughts:

Because It Is Getting Better

Date: Mood:

Today I Felt: Today I Needed:

Today I Was Triggered By (Answer If   Tommorow I Will Challenge Myself:
Applicable):

Who And/Or What Triggered Me   What Do I Forgive About The Past?
(Answer If Applicable)?

How Did I Respond To My Tigger Today   By Forgiving I Am:
(Answer If Applicable)?

How Did I Make My Trigger Powerless   Today I Stopped/Started/Maintained:
Today?

How Was I Present Today?   How Can I Retell The Story Of A Past
                                             Traumatic Event?

What Thoughts Did I Dwell On That I   I Lct Go In Trying To Find The Answer/
Needed To Stop Thinking About That   Reason To:
Caused Unwanted Feelings?

Today I Realized: Tonight's Thoughts:

I Am Taking It A Day At A Time.

My Safe Space Looks And Feels....

Because It Is Getting Better

Date: Mood:

Today I Felt: Today I Needed:

Today I Was Triggered By (Answer If   Tommorow I Will Challenge Myself:
Applicable):

Who And/Or What Triggered Me   What Do I Forgive About The Past?
(Answer If Applicable)?

How Did I Respond To My Tigger Today   By Forgiving I Am:
(Answer If Applicable)?

How Did I Make My Trigger Powerless   Today I Stopped/Started/Maintained:
Today?

How Was I Present Today?   How Can I Retell The Story Of A Past
                                               Traumatic Event?

What Thoughts Did I Dwell On That I   I Let Go In Trying To Find The Answer/
Needed To Stop Thinking About That   Reason To:
Caused Unwanted Feelings?

Today I Realized: Tonight's Thoughts:

Because It Is Getting Better

Date: Mood:

Today I Felt: Today I Needed:

Today I Was Triggered By (Answer If   Tommorow I Will Challenge Myself:
Applicable):

Who And/Or What Triggered Me   What Do I Forgive About The Past?
(Answer If Applicable)?

How Did I Respond To My Tigger Today   By Forgiving I Am:
(Answer If Applicable)?

How Did I Make My Trigger Powerless   Today I Stopped/Started/Maintained:
Today?

How Was I Present Today?   How Can I Retell The Story Of A Past
                                                Traumatic Event?

What Thoughts Did I Dwell On That I   I Let Go In Trying To Find The Answer/
Needed To Stop Thinking About That   Reason To:
Caused Unwanted Feelings?

Today I Realized: Tonight's Thoughts:

Because It Is Getting Better

Date: Mood:

Today I Felt: Today I Needed:

Today I Was Triggered By (Answer If   Tommorow I Will Challenge Myself:
Applicable):

Who And/Or What Triggered Me   What Do I Forgive About The Past?
(Answer If Applicable)?

How Did I Respond To My Tigger Today   By Forgiving I Am:
(Answer If Applicable)?

How Did I Make My Trigger Powerless   Today I Stopped/Started/Maintained:
Today?

How Was I Present Today?   How Can I Retell The Story Of A Past
                                                Traumatic Event?

What Thoughts Did I Dwell On That I   I Let Go In Trying To Find The Answer/
Needed To Stop Thinking About That   Reason To:
Caused Unwanted Feelings?

Today I Realized: Tonight's Thoughts:

I Have Struggled. I Have Conquered.

Because It Is Getting Better

Date: Mood:

Today I Felt: Today I Needed:

Today I Was Triggered By (Answer If   Tommorow I Will Challenge Myself:
Applicable):

Who And/Or What Triggered Me   What Do I Forgive About The Past?
(Answer If Applicable)?

How Did I Respond To My Tigger Today   By Forgiving I Am:
(Answer If Applicable)?

How Did I Make My Trigger Powerless   Today I Stopped/Started/Maintained:
Today?

How Was I Present Today?   How Can I Retell The Story Of A Past
                                               Traumatic Event?

What Thoughts Did I Dwell On That I   I Let Go In Trying To Find The Answer/
Needed To Stop Thinking About That   Reason To:
Caused Unwanted Feelings?

Today I Realized: Tonight's Thoughts:

Because It Is Getting Better

Date: Mood:

Today I Felt: Today I Needed:

Today I Was Triggered By (Answer If   Tommorow I Will Challenge Myself:
Applicable):

Who And/Or What Triggered Me   What Do I Forgive About The Past?
(Answer If Applicable)?

How Did I Respond To My Tigger Today   By Forgiving I Am:
(Answer If Applicable)?

How Did I Make My Trigger Powerless   Today I Stopped/Started/Maintained:
Today?

How Was I Present Today?   How Can I Retell The Story Of A Past
                                                Traumatic Event?

What Thoughts Did I Dwell On That I   I Let Go In Trying To Find The Answer/
Needed To Stop Thinking About That   Reason To:
Caused Unwanted Feelings?

Today I Realized: Tonight's Thoughts:

New Boundaries.
Higher
Levels Of
Love.
-Me

My Personal Thoughts

No Maybes. I Am Just Saying No.

Because It Is Getting Better

Date: Mood:

Today I Felt: Today I Needed:

Today I Was Triggered By (Answer If   Tommorow I Will Challenge Myself:
Applicable):

Who And/Or What Triggered Me   What Do I Forgive About The Past?
(Answer If Applicable)?

How Did I Respond To My Tigger Today   By Forgiving I Am:
(Answer If Applicable)?

How Did I Make My Trigger Powerless   Today I Stopped/Started/Maintained:
Today?

How Was I Present Today?   How Can I Retell The Story Of A Past
                                              Traumatic Event?

What Thoughts Did I Dwell On That I   I Let Go In Trying To Find The Answer/
Needed To Stop Thinking About That   Reason To:
Caused Unwanted Feelings?

Today I Realized: Tonight's Thoughts:

Because It Is Getting Better

Date: Mood:

Today I Felt: Today I Needed:

Today I Was Triggered By (Answer If   Tommorow I Will Challenge Myself:
Applicable):

Who And/Or What Triggered Me   What Do I Forgive About The Past?
(Answer If Applicable)?

How Did I Respond To My Tigger Today   By Forgiving I Am:
(Answer If Applicable)?

How Did I Make My Trigger Powerless   Today I Stopped/Started/Maintained:
Today?

How Was I Present Today?   How Can I Retell The Story Of A Past
                                                Traumatic Event?

What Thoughts Did I Dwell On That I   I Let Go In Trying To Find The Answer/
Needed To Stop Thinking About That   Reason To:
Caused Unwanted Feelings?

Today I Realized: Tonight's Thoughts:

Because It Is Getting Better

Date: Mood:

Today I Felt: Today I Needed:

Today I Was Triggered By (Answer If   Tommorow I Will Challenge Myself:
Applicable):

Who And/Or What Triggered Me   What Do I Forgive About The Past?
(Answer If Applicable)?

How Did I Respond To My Tigger Today   By Forgiving I Am:
(Answer If Applicable)?

How Did I Make My Trigger Powerless   Today I Stopped/Started/Maintained:
Today?

How Was I Present Today?   How Can I Retell The Story Of A Past
                                         Traumatic Event?

What Thoughts Did I Dwell On That I   I Let Go In Trying To Find The Answer/
Needed To Stop Thinking About That   Reason To:
Caused Unwanted Feelings?

Today I Realized: Tonight's Thoughts:

Because It Is Getting Better

Date: Mood:

Today I Felt: Today I Needed:

Today I Was Triggered By (Answer If   Tommorow I Will Challenge Myself:
Applicable):

Who And/Or What Triggered Me   What Do I Forgive About The Past?
(Answer If Applicable)?

How Did I Respond To My Tigger Today   By Forgiving I Am:
(Answer If Applicable)?

How Did I Make My Trigger Powerless   Today I Stopped/Started/Maintained:
Today?

How Was I Present Today?   How Can I Retell The Story Of A Past
                                           Traumatic Event?

What Thoughts Did I Dwell On That I   I Let Go In Trying To Find The Answer/
Needed To Stop Thinking About That   Reason To:
Caused Unwanted Feelings?

Today I Realized: Tonight's Thoughts:

What Happened To Me Will Not Stop Me From Opening Up My Heart Again.

It May Not Happen Overnight, But With Time I Am Choosing To Heal.

Because It Is Getting Better

Date: Mood:

Today I Felt: Today I Needed:

Today I Was Triggered By (Answer If   Tommorow I Will Challenge Myself:
Applicable):

Who And/Or What Triggered Me   What Do I Forgive About The Past?
(Answer If Applicable)?

How Did I Respond To My Tigger Today   By Forgiving I Am:
(Answer If Applicable)?

How Did I Make My Trigger Powerless   Today I Stopped/Started/Maintained:
Today?

How Was I Present Today?   How Can I Retell The Story Of A Past
                                               Traumatic Event?

What Thoughts Did I Dwell On That I   I Let Go In Trying To Find The Answer/
Needed To Stop Thinking About That   Reason To:
Caused Unwanted Feelings?

Today I Realized: Tonight's Thoughts:

Because It Is Getting Better

Date: Mood:

Today I Felt: Today I Needed:

Today I Was Triggered By (Answer If   Tommorow I Will Challenge Myself:
Applicable):

Who And/Or What Triggered Me   What Do I Forgive About The Past?
(Answer If Applicable)?

How Did I Respond To My Tigger Today   By Forgiving I Am:
(Answer If Applicable)?

How Did I Make My Trigger Powerless   Today I Stopped/Started/Maintained:
Today?

How Was I Present Today?   How Can I Retell The Story Of A Past
                                                    Traumatic Event?

What Thoughts Did I Dwell On That I   I Let Go In Trying To Find The Answer/
Needed To Stop Thinking About That   Reason To:
Caused Unwanted Feelings?

Today I Realized: Tonight's Thoughts:

I Feel At Peace When....

Because It Is Getting Better

Date: Mood:

Today I Felt: Today I Needed:

Today I Was Triggered By (Answer If   Tommorow I Will Challenge Myself:
Applicable):

Who And/Or What Triggered Me   What Do I Forgive About The Past?
(Answer If Applicable)?

How Did I Respond To My Tigger Today   By Forgiving I Am:
(Answer If Applicable)?

How Did I Make My Trigger Powerless   Today I Stopped/Started/Maintained:
Today?

How Was I Present Today?   How Can I Retell The Story Of A Past
                                        Traumatic Event?

What Thoughts Did I Dwell On That I   I Let Go In Trying To Find The Answer/
Needed To Stop Thinking About That   Reason To:
Caused Unwanted Feelings?

Today I Realized: Tonight's Thoughts:

Because It Is Getting Better

Date: Mood:

Today I Felt: Today I Needed:

Today I Was Triggered By (Answer If   Tommorow I Will Challenge Myself:
Applicable):

Who And/Or What Triggered Me   What Do I Forgive About The Past?
(Answer If Applicable)?

How Did I Respond To My Tigger Today   By Forgiving I Am:
(Answer If Applicable)?

How Did I Make My Trigger Powerless   Today I Stopped/Started/Maintained:
Today?

How Was I Present Today?   How Can I Retell The Story Of A Past
                                         Traumatic Event?

What Thoughts Did I Dwell On That I   I Let Go In Trying To Find The Answer/
Needed To Stop Thinking About That   Reason To:
Caused Unwanted Feelings?

Today I Realized: Tonight's Thoughts:

Because It Is Getting Better

Date: Mood:

Today I Felt: Today I Needed:

Today I Was Triggered By (Answer If   Tommorow I Will Challenge Myself:
Applicable):

Who And/Or What Triggered Me   What Do I Forgive About The Past?
(Answer If Applicable)?

How Did I Respond To My Tigger Today   By Forgiving I Am:
(Answer If Applicable)?

How Did I Make My Trigger Powerless   Today I Stopped/Started/Maintained:
Today?

How Was I Present Today?   How Can I Retell The Story Of A Past
                                               Traumatic Event?

What Thoughts Did I Dwell On That I   I Let Go In Trying To Find The Answer/
Needed To Stop Thinking About That   Reason To:
Caused Unwanted Feelings?

Today I Realized: Tonight's Thoughts:

My Personal Thoughts

I Am Not What You Are Use To.

Because It Is Getting Better

Date: | Mood:

Today I Felt: | Today I Needed:

Today I Was Triggered By (Answer If Applicable): | Tommorow I Will Challenge Myself:

Who And/Or What Triggered Me (Answer If Applicable)? | What Do I Forgive About The Past?

How Did I Respond To My Tigger Today (Answer If Applicable)? | By Forgiving I Am:

How Did I Make My Trigger Powerless Today? | Today I Stopped/Started/Maintained:

How Was I Present Today? | How Can I Retell The Story Of A Past Traumatic Event?

What Thoughts Did I Dwell On That I Needed To Stop Thinking About That Caused Unwanted Feelings? | I Let Go In Trying To Find The Answer/ Reason To:

Today I Realized: | Tonight's Thoughts:

Because It Is Getting Better

Date: Mood:

Today I Felt: Today I Needed:

Today I Was Triggered By (Answer If   Tommorow I Will Challenge Myself:
Applicable):

Who And/Or What Triggered Me   What Do I Forgive About The Past?
(Answer If Applicable)?

How Did I Respond To My Tigger Today   By Forgiving I Am:
(Answer If Applicable)?

How Did I Make My Trigger Powerless   Today I Stopped/Started/Maintained:
Today?

How Was I Present Today?   How Can I Retell The Story Of A Past
                                         Traumatic Event?

What Thoughts Did I Dwell On That I   I Let Go In Trying To Find The Answer/
Needed To Stop Thinking About That   Reason To:
Caused Unwanted Feelings?

Today I Realized: Tonight's Thoughts:

Because It Is Getting Better

Date: Mood:

Today I Felt: Today I Needed:

Today I Was Triggered By (Answer If   Tommorow I Will Challenge Myself:
Applicable):

Who And/Or What Triggered Me   What Do I Forgive About The Past?
(Answer If Applicable)?

How Did I Respond To My Tigger Today   By Forgiving I Am:
(Answer If Applicable)?

How Did I Make My Trigger Powerless   Today I Stopped/Started/Maintained:
Today?

How Was I Present Today?   How Can I Retell The Story Of A Past
                                               Traumatic Event?

What Thoughts Did I Dwell On That I   I Let Go In Trying To Find The Answer/
Needed To Stop Thinking About That   Reason To:
Caused Unwanted Feelings?

Today I Realized: Tonight's Thoughts:

My Personal Thoughts

That Situation Exposed Me To Who Was And Still Is There For Me.

Because It Is Getting Better

Date: Mood:

Today I Felt: Today I Needed:

Today I Was Triggered By (Answer If   Tommorow I Will Challenge Myself:
Applicable):

Who And/Or What Triggered Me   What Do I Forgive About The Past?
(Answer If Applicable)?

How Did I Respond To My Tigger Today   By Forgiving I Am:
(Answer If Applicable)?

How Did I Make My Trigger Powerless   Today I Stopped/Started/Maintained:
Today?

How Was I Present Today?   How Can I Retell The Story Of A Past
                                                Traumatic Event?

What Thoughts Did I Dwell On That I   I Let Go In Trying To Find The Answer/
Needed To Stop Thinking About That   Reason To:
Caused Unwanted Feelings?

Today I Realized: Tonight's Thoughts:

Because It Is Getting Better

Date: Mood:

Today I Felt: Today I Needed:

Today I Was Triggered By (Answer If   Tommorow I Will Challenge Myself:
Applicable):

Who And/Or What Triggered Me   What Do I Forgive About The Past?
(Answer If Applicable)?

How Did I Respond To My Tigger Today   By Forgiving I Am:
(Answer If Applicable)?

How Did I Make My Trigger Powerless   Today I Stopped/Started/Maintained:
Today?

How Was I Present Today?   How Can I Retell The Story Of A Past
                                               Traumatic Event?

What Thoughts Did I Dwell On That I   I Let Go In Trying To Find The Answer/
Needed To Stop Thinking About That   Reason To:
Caused Unwanted Feelings?

Today I Realized: Tonight's Thoughts:

Five Songs That Make Me Feel Happy....

1.

2.

3.

4.

5.

Because It Is Getting Better

Date: Mood:

Today I Felt: Today I Needed:

Today I Was Triggered By (Answer If   Tommorow I Will Challenge Myself:
Applicable):

Who And/Or What Triggered Me   What Do I Forgive About The Past?
(Answer If Applicable)?

How Did I Respond To My Tigger Today   By Forgiving I Am:
(Answer If Applicable)?

How Did I Make My Trigger Powerless   Today I Stopped/Started/Maintained:
Today?

How Was I Present Today?   How Can I Retell The Story Of A Past
                                           Traumatic Event?

What Thoughts Did I Dwell On That I   I Let Go In Trying To Find The Answer/
Needed To Stop Thinking About That   Reason To:
Caused Unwanted Feelings?

Today I Realized: Tonight's Thoughts:

My Personal Thoughts

I Grew Stronger.

Because It Is Getting Better

Date: Mood:

Today I Felt: Today I Needed:

Today I Was Triggered By (Answer If   Tommorow I Will Challenge Myself:
Applicable):

Who And/Or What Triggered Me   What Do I Forgive About The Past?
(Answer If Applicable)?

How Did I Respond To My Tigger Today   By Forgiving I Am:
(Answer If Applicable)?

How Did I Make My Trigger Powerless   Today I Stopped/Started/Maintained:
Today?

How Was I Present Today?   How Can I Retell The Story Of A Past
                                               Traumatic Event?

What Thoughts Did I Dwell On That I   I Let Go In Trying To Find The Answer/
Needed To Stop Thinking About That   Reason To:
Caused Unwanted Feelings?

Today I Realized: Tonight's Thoughts:

Because It Is Getting Better

Date: Mood:

Today I Felt: Today I Needed:

Today I Was Triggered By (Answer If   Tommorow I Will Challenge Myself:
Applicable):

Who And/Or What Triggered Me   What Do I Forgive About The Past?
(Answer If Applicable)?

How Did I Respond To My Tigger Today   By Forgiving I Am:
(Answer If Applicable)?

How Did I Make My Trigger Powerless   Today I Stopped/Started/Maintained:
Today?

How Was I Present Today?   How Can I Retell The Story Of A Past
                                               Traumatic Event?

What Thoughts Did I Dwell On That I   I Let Go In Trying To Find The Answer/
Needed To Stop Thinking About That   Reason To:
Caused Unwanted Feelings?

Today I Realized: Tonight's Thoughts:

Because It Is Getting Better

Date: Mood:

Today I Felt: Today I Needed:

Today I Was Triggered By (Answer If   Tommorow I Will Challenge Myself:
Applicable):

Who And/Or What Triggered Me   What Do I Forgive About The Past?
(Answer If Applicable)?

How Did I Respond To My Tigger Today   By Forgiving I Am:
(Answer If Applicable)?

How Did I Make My Trigger Powerless   Today I Stopped/Started/Maintained:
Today?

How Was I Present Today?   How Can I Retell The Story Of A Past
                                               Traumatic Event?

What Thoughts Did I Dwell On That I   I Let Go In Trying To Find The Answer/
Needed To Stop Thinking About That   Reason To:
Caused Unwanted Feelings?

Today I Realized: Tonight's Thoughts:

Because It Is Getting Better

Date: Mood:

Today I Felt: Today I Needed:

Today I Was Triggered By (Answer If   Tommorow I Will Challenge Myself:
Applicable):

Who And/Or What Triggered Me   What Do I Forgive About The Past?
(Answer If Applicable)?

How Did I Respond To My Tigger Today   By Forgiving I Am:
(Answer If Applicable)?

How Did I Make My Trigger Powerless   Today I Stopped/Started/Maintained:
Today?

How Was I Present Today?   How Can I Retell The Story Of A Past
                                             Traumatic Event?

What Thoughts Did I Dwell On That I   I Let Go In Trying To Find The Answer/
Needed To Stop Thinking About That   Reason To:
Caused Unwanted Feelings?

Today I Realized: Tonight's Thoughts:

God Is With Me.

My Personal Thoughts

Because It Is Getting Better

Date: Mood:

Today I Felt: Today I Needed:

Today I Was Triggered By (Answer If   Tommorow I Will Challenge Myself:
Applicable):

Who And/Or What Triggered Me   What Do I Forgive About The Past?
(Answer If Applicable)?

How Did I Respond To My Tigger Today   By Forgiving I Am:
(Answer If Applicable)?

How Did I Make My Trigger Powerless   Today I Stopped/Started/Maintained:
Today?

How Was I Present Today?   How Can I Retell The Story Of A Past
                                         Traumatic Event?

What Thoughts Did I Dwell On That I   I Let Go In Trying To Find The Answer/
Needed To Stop Thinking About That   Reason To:
Caused Unwanted Feelings?

Today I Realized: Tonight's Thoughts:

Because It Is Getting Better

Date: Mood:

Today I Felt: Today I Needed:

Today I Was Triggered By (Answer If   Tommorow I Will Challenge Myself:
Applicable):

Who And/Or What Triggered Me   What Do I Forgive About The Past?
(Answer If Applicable)?

How Did I Respond To My Tigger Today   By Forgiving I Am:
(Answer If Applicable)?

How Did I Make My Trigger Powerless   Today I Stopped/Started/Maintained:
Today?

How Was I Present Today?   How Can I Retell The Story Of A Past
                                         Traumatic Event?

What Thoughts Did I Dwell On That I   I Let Go In Trying To Find The Answer/
Needed To Stop Thinking About That   Reason To:
Caused Unwanted Feelings?

Today I Realized: Tonight's Thoughts:

A Bad Experience Does Not Make It A Bad Life.

Who Can I Be There For?

Because It Is Getting Better

Date: Mood:

Today I Felt: Today I Needed:

Today I Was Triggered By (Answer If   Tommorow I Will Challenge Myself:
Applicable):

Who And/Or What Triggered Me   What Do I Forgive About The Past?
(Answer If Applicable)?

How Did I Respond To My Tigger Today   By Forgiving I Am:
(Answer If Applicable)?

How Did I Make My Trigger Powerless   Today I Stopped/Started/Maintained:
Today?

How Was I Present Today?   How Can I Retell The Story Of A Past
                                         Traumatic Event?

What Thoughts Did I Dwell On That I   I Let Go In Trying To Find The Answer/
Needed To Stop Thinking About That   Reason To:
Caused Unwanted Feelings?

Today I Realized: Tonight's Thoughts:

I See Things Differently Now.

I Will Never Forget Who I Am.

Because It Is Getting Better

Date: Mood:

Today I Felt: Today I Needed:

Today I Was Triggered By (Answer If   Tommorow I Will Challenge Myself:
Applicable):

Who And/Or What Triggered Me   What Do I Forgive About The Past?
(Answer If Applicable)?

How Did I Respond To My Tigger Today   By Forgiving I Am:
(Answer If Applicable)?

How Did I Make My Trigger Powerless   Today I Stopped/Started/Maintained:
Today?

How Was I Present Today?   How Can I Retell The Story Of A Past
                                               Traumatic Event?

What Thoughts Did I Dwell On That I   I Let Go In Trying To Find The Answer/
Needed To Stop Thinking About That   Reason To:
Caused Unwanted Feelings?

Today I Realized: Tonight's Thoughts:

Because It Is Getting Better

Date: Mood:

Today I Felt: Today I Needed:

Today I Was Triggered By (Answer If   Tommorow I Will Challenge Myself:
Applicable):

Who And/Or What Triggered Me   What Do I Forgive About The Past?
(Answer If Applicable)?

How Did I Respond To My Tigger Today   By Forgiving I Am:
(Answer If Applicable)?

How Did I Make My Trigger Powerless   Today I Stopped/Started/Maintained:
Today?

How Was I Present Today?   How Can I Retell The Story Of A Past
                                               Traumatic Event?

What Thoughts Did I Dwell On That I   I Let Go In Trying To Find The Answer/
Needed To Stop Thinking About That   Reason To:
Caused Unwanted Feelings?

Today I Realized: Tonight's Thoughts:

My Personal Thoughts

Because It Is Getting Better

Date: Mood:

Today I Felt: Today I Needed:

Today I Was Triggered By (Answer If   Tommorow I Will Challenge Myself:
Applicable):

Who And/Or What Triggered Me   What Do I Forgive About The Past?
(Answer If Applicable)?

How Did I Respond To My Tigger Today   By Forgiving I Am:
(Answer If Applicable)?

How Did I Make My Trigger Powerless   Today I Stopped/Started/Maintained:
Today?

How Was I Present Today?   How Can I Retell The Story Of A Past
                                               Traumatic Event?

What Thoughts Did I Dwell On That I   I Let Go In Trying To Find The Answer/
Needed To Stop Thinking About That   Reason To:
Caused Unwanted Feelings?

Today I Realized: Tonight's Thoughts:

Because It Is Getting Better

Date: Mood:

Today I Felt: Today I Needed:

Today I Was Triggered By (Answer If   Tommorow I Will Challenge Myself:
Applicable):

Who And/Or What Triggered Me   What Do I Forgive About The Past?
(Answer If Applicable)?

How Did I Respond To My Tigger Today   By Forgiving I Am:
(Answer If Applicable)?

How Did I Make My Trigger Powerless   Today I Stopped/Started/Maintained:
Today?

How Was I Present Today?   How Can I Retell The Story Of A Past
                                         Traumatic Event?

What Thoughts Did I Dwell On That I   I Let Go In Trying To Find The Answer/
Needed To Stop Thinking About That   Reason To:
Caused Unwanted Feelings?

Today I Realized: Tonight's Thoughts:

As Soon As I Think About My Trauma, I Make An Effort To Improve My Thoughts By....

My Actions Prove Who I Am And My Words Prove Who I Want To Be.

I Am Not Defined By This.

Because It Is Getting Better

Date: Mood:

Today I Felt: Today I Needed:

Today I Was Triggered By (Answer If Applicable):   Tommorow I Will Challenge Myself:

Who And/Or What Triggered Me (Answer If Applicable)?   What Do I Forgive About The Past?

How Did I Respond To My Tigger Today (Answer If Applicable)?   By Forgiving I Am:

How Did I Make My Trigger Powerless Today?   Today I Stopped/Started/Maintained:

How Was I Present Today?   How Can I Retell The Story Of A Past Traumatic Event?

What Thoughts Did I Dwell On That I Needed To Stop Thinking About That Caused Unwanted Feelings?   I Let Go In Trying To Find The Answer/ Reason To:

Today I Realized: Tonight's Thoughts:

I Forgive You.

Because It Is Getting Better

Date: Mood:

Today I Felt: Today I Needed:

Today I Was Triggered By (Answer If   Tommorow I Will Challenge Myself:
Applicable):

Who And/Or What Triggered Me   What Do I Forgive About The Past?
(Answer If Applicable)?

How Did I Respond To My Tigger Today   By Forgiving I Am:
(Answer If Applicable)?

How Did I Make My Trigger Powerless   Today I Stopped/Started/Maintained:
Today?

How Was I Present Today?   How Can I Retell The Story Of A Past
                                         Traumatic Event?

What Thoughts Did I Dwell On That I   I Let Go In Trying To Find The Answer/
Needed To Stop Thinking About That   Reason To:
Caused Unwanted Feelings?

Today I Realized: Tonight's Thoughts:

Because It Is Getting Better

Date: Mood:

Today I Felt: Today I Needed:

Today I Was Triggered By (Answer If   Tommorow I Will Challenge Myself:
Applicable):

Who And/Or What Triggered Me   What Do I Forgive About The Past?
(Answer If Applicable)?

How Did I Respond To My Tigger Today   By Forgiving I Am:
(Answer If Applicable)?

How Did I Make My Trigger Powerless   Today I Stopped/Started/Maintained:
Today?

How Was I Present Today?   How Can I Retell The Story Of A Past
                                               Traumatic Event?

What Thoughts Did I Dwell On That I   I Let Go In Trying To Find The Answer/
Needed To Stop Thinking About That   Reason To:
Caused Unwanted Feelings?

Today I Realized: Tonight's Thoughts:

Because It Is Getting Better

Date: Mood:

Today I Felt: Today I Needed:

Today I Was Triggered By (Answer If   Tommorow I Will Challenge Myself:
Applicable):

Who And/Or What Triggered Me   What Do I Forgive About The Past?
(Answer If Applicable)?

How Did I Respond To My Tigger Today   By Forgiving I Am:
(Answer If Applicable)?

How Did I Make My Trigger Powerless   Today I Stopped/Started/Maintained:
Today?

How Was I Present Today?   How Can I Retell The Story Of A Past
                                               Traumatic Event?

What Thoughts Did I Dwell On That I   I Let Go In Trying To Find The Answer/
Needed To Stop Thinking About That   Reason To:
Caused Unwanted Feelings?

Today I Realized: Tonight's Thoughts:

My Personal Thoughts

I Will Not Allow Anyone To Touch My Spirit.

Because It Is Getting Better

Date: Mood:

Today I Felt: Today I Needed:

Today I Was Triggered By (Answer If   Tommorow I Will Challenge Myself:
Applicable):

Who And/Or What Triggered Me   What Do I Forgive About The Past?
(Answer If Applicable)?

How Did I Respond To My Tigger Today   By Forgiving I Am:
(Answer If Applicable)?

How Did I Make My Trigger Powerless   Today I Stopped/Started/Maintained:
Today?

How Was I Present Today?   How Can I Retell The Story Of A Past
                                               Traumatic Event?

What Thoughts Did I Dwell On That I   I Let Go In Trying To Find The Answer/
Needed To Stop Thinking About That   Reason To:
Caused Unwanted Feelings?

Today I Realized: Tonight's Thoughts:

Because It Is Getting Better

Date: Mood:

Today I Felt: Today I Needed:

Today I Was Triggered By (Answer If   Tommorow I Will Challenge Myself:
Applicable):

Who And/Or What Triggered Me   What Do I Forgive About The Past?
(Answer If Applicable)?

How Did I Respond To My Tigger Today   By Forgiving I Am:
(Answer If Applicable)?

How Did I Make My Trigger Powerless   Today I Stopped/Started/Maintained:
Today?

How Was I Present Today?   How Can I Retell The Story Of A Past
                                               Traumatic Event?

What Thoughts Did I Dwell On That I   I Let Go In Trying To Find The Answer/
Needed To Stop Thinking About That   Reason To:
Caused Unwanted Feelings?

Today I Realized: Tonight's Thoughts:

Because It Is Getting Better

Date: Mood:

Today I Felt: Today I Needed:

Today I Was Triggered By (Answer If   Tommorow I Will Challenge Myself:
Applicable):

Who And/Or What Triggered Me   What Do I Forgive About The Past?
(Answer If Applicable)?

How Did I Respond To My Tigger Today   By Forgiving I Am:
(Answer If Applicable)?

How Did I Make My Trigger Powerless   Today I Stopped/Started/Maintained:
Today?

How Was I Present Today?   How Can I Retell The Story Of A Past
                                                Traumatic Event?

What Thoughts Did I Dwell On That I   I Let Go In Trying To Find The Answer/
Needed To Stop Thinking About That   Reason To:
Caused Unwanted Feelings?

Today I Realized: Tonight's Thoughts:

I Made It Through The Fire.

I Will Only Entertain Thoughts That Empower Me.

Because It Is Getting Better

Date: Mood:

Today I Felt: Today I Needed:

Today I Was Triggered By (Answer If   Tommorow I Will Challenge Myself:
Applicable):

Who And/Or What Triggered Me   What Do I Forgive About The Past?
(Answer If Applicable)?

How Did I Respond To My Tigger Today   By Forgiving I Am:
(Answer If Applicable)?

How Did I Make My Trigger Powerless   Today I Stopped/Started/Maintained:
Today?

How Was I Present Today?   How Can I Retell The Story Of A Past
                                                         Traumatic Event?

What Thoughts Did I Dwell On That I   I Let Go In Trying To Find The Answer/
Needed To Stop Thinking About That   Reason To:
Caused Unwanted Feelings?

Today I Realized: Tonight's Thoughts:

Because It Is Getting Better

Date: Mood:

Today I Felt: Today I Needed:

Today I Was Triggered By (Answer If   Tommorow I Will Challenge Myself:
Applicable):

Who And/Or What Triggered Me   What Do I Forgive About The Past?
(Answer If Applicable)?

How Did I Respond To My Tigger Today   By Forgiving I Am:
(Answer If Applicable)?

How Did I Make My Trigger Powerless   Today I Stopped/Started/Maintained:
Today?

How Was I Present Today?   How Can I Retell The Story Of A Past
                                               Traumatic Event?

What Thoughts Did I Dwell On That I   I Let Go In Trying To Find The Answer/
Needed To Stop Thinking About That   Reason To:
Caused Unwanted Feelings?

Today I Realized: Tonight's Thoughts:

My Personal Thoughts

Because It Is Getting Better

Date: Mood:

Today I Felt: Today I Needed:

Today I Was Triggered By (Answer If   Tommorow I Will Challenge Myself:
Applicable):

Who And/Or What Triggered Me   What Do I Forgive About The Past?
(Answer If Applicable)?

How Did I Respond To My Tigger Today   By Forgiving I Am:
(Answer If Applicable)?

How Did I Make My Trigger Powerless   Today I Stopped/Started/Maintained:
Today?

How Was I Present Today?   How Can I Retell The Story Of A Past
                                                    Traumatic Event?

What Thoughts Did I Dwell On That I   I Let Go In Trying To Find The Answer/
Needed To Stop Thinking About That   Reason To:
Caused Unwanted Feelings?

Today I Realized: Tonight's Thoughts:

Because It Is Getting Better

Date: Mood:

Today I Felt: Today I Needed:

Today I Was Triggered By (Answer If   Tommorow I Will Challenge Myself:
Applicable):

Who And/Or What Triggered Me   What Do I Forgive About The Past?
(Answer If Applicable)?

How Did I Respond To My Tigger Today   By Forgiving I Am:
(Answer If Applicable)?

How Did I Make My Trigger Powerless   Today I Stopped/Started/Maintained:
Today?

How Was I Present Today?   How Can I Retell The Story Of A Past
                                             Traumatic Event?

What Thoughts Did I Dwell On That I   I Let Go In Trying To Find The Answer/
Needed To Stop Thinking About That   Reason To:
Caused Unwanted Feelings?

Today I Realized: Tonight's Thoughts:

Counting My Blessings.

I Know I Would Feel Better....

Because It Is Getting Better

Date: Mood:

Today I Felt: Today I Needed:

Today I Was Triggered By (Answer If   Tommorow I Will Challenge Myself:
Applicable):

Who And/Or What Triggered Me   What Do I Forgive About The Past?
(Answer If Applicable)?

How Did I Respond To My Tigger Today   By Forgiving I Am:
(Answer If Applicable)?

How Did I Make My Trigger Powerless   Today I Stopped/Started/Maintained:
Today?

How Was I Present Today?   How Can I Retell The Story Of A Past
                                               Traumatic Event?

What Thoughts Did I Dwell On That I   I Let Go In Trying To Find The Answer/
Needed To Stop Thinking About That   Reason To:
Caused Unwanted Feelings?

Today I Realized: Tonight's Thoughts:

Because It Is Getting Better

Date: Mood:

Today I Felt: Today I Needed:

Today I Was Triggered By (Answer If   Tommorow I Will Challenge Myself:
Applicable):

Who And/Or What Triggered Me   What Do I Forgive About The Past?
(Answer If Applicable)?

How Did I Respond To My Tigger Today   By Forgiving I Am:
(Answer If Applicable)?

How Did I Make My Trigger Powerless   Today I Stopped/Started/Maintained:
Today?

How Was I Present Today?   How Can I Retell The Story Of A Past
                                               Traumatic Event?

What Thoughts Did I Dwell On That I   I Let Go In Trying To Find The Answer/
Needed To Stop Thinking About That   Reason To:
Caused Unwanted Feelings?

Today I Realized: Tonight's Thoughts:

My Personal Thoughts

Because It Is Getting Better

Date: Mood:

Today I Felt: Today I Needed:

Today I Was Triggered By (Answer If   Tommorow I Will Challenge Myself:
Applicable):

Who And/Or What Triggered Me   What Do I Forgive About The Past?
(Answer If Applicable)?

How Did I Respond To My Tigger Today   By Forgiving I Am:
(Answer If Applicable)?

How Did I Make My Trigger Powerless   Today I Stopped/Started/Maintained:
Today?

How Was I Present Today?   How Can I Retell The Story Of A Past
                                               Traumatic Event?

What Thoughts Did I Dwell On That I   I Let Go In Trying To Find The Answer/
Needed To Stop Thinking About That   Reason To:
Caused Unwanted Feelings?

Today I Realized: Tonight's Thoughts:

Because It Is Getting Better

Date: Mood:

Today I Felt: Today I Needed:

Today I Was Triggered By (Answer If   Tommorow I Will Challenge Myself:
Applicable):

Who And/Or What Triggered Me   What Do I Forgive About The Past?
(Answer If Applicable)?

How Did I Respond To My Tigger Today   By Forgiving I Am:
(Answer If Applicable)?

How Did I Make My Trigger Powerless   Today I Stopped/Started/Maintained:
Today?

How Was I Present Today?   How Can I Retell The Story Of A Past
                                                Traumatic Event?

What Thoughts Did I Dwell On That I   I Let Go In Trying To Find The Answer/
Needed To Stop Thinking About That   Reason To:
Caused Unwanted Feelings?

Today I Realized: Tonight's Thoughts:

Because It Is Getting Better

Date: Mood:

Today I Felt: Today I Needed:

Today I Was Triggered By (Answer If Applicable):   Tommorow I Will Challenge Myself:

Who And/Or What Triggered Me (Answer If Applicable)?   What Do I Forgive About The Past?

How Did I Respond To My Tigger Today (Answer If Applicable)?   By Forgiving I Am:

How Did I Make My Trigger Powerless Today?   Today I Stopped/Started/Maintained:

How Was I Present Today?   How Can I Retell The Story Of A Past Traumatic Event?

What Thoughts Did I Dwell On That I Needed To Stop Thinking About That Caused Unwanted Feelings?   I Let Go In Trying To Find The Answer/Reason To:

Today I Realized: Tonight's Thoughts:

249

Letting Go Of What I Cannot Control.

Because It Is Getting Better

Date: Mood:

Today I Felt: Today I Needed:

Today I Was Triggered By (Answer If   Tommorow I Will Challenge Myself:
Applicable):

Who And/Or What Triggered Me   What Do I Forgive About The Past?
(Answer If Applicable)?

How Did I Respond To My Tigger Today   By Forgiving I Am:
(Answer If Applicable)?

How Did I Make My Trigger Powerless   Today I Stopped/Started/Maintained:
Today?

How Was I Present Today?   How Can I Retell The Story Of A Past
                                               Traumatic Event?

What Thoughts Did I Dwell On That I   I Let Go In Trying To Find The Answer/
Needed To Stop Thinking About That   Reason To:
Caused Unwanted Feelings?

Today I Realized: Tonight's Thoughts:

Because It Is Getting Better

Date: Mood:

Today I Felt: Today I Needed:

Today I Was Triggered By (Answer If   Tommorow I Will Challenge Myself:
Applicable):

Who And/Or What Triggered Me   What Do I Forgive About The Past?
(Answer If Applicable)?

How Did I Respond To My Tigger Today   By Forgiving I Am:
(Answer If Applicable)?

How Did I Make My Trigger Powerless   Today I Stopped/Started/Maintained:
Today?

How Was I Present Today?   How Can I Retell The Story Of A Past
                                         Traumatic Event?

What Thoughts Did I Dwell On That I   I Let Go In Trying To Find The Answer/
Needed To Stop Thinking About That   Reason To:
Caused Unwanted Feelings?

Today I Realized: Tonight's Thoughts:

Because It Is Getting Better

Date: Mood:

Today I Felt: Today I Needed:

Today I Was Triggered By (Answer If   Tommorow I Will Challenge Myself:
Applicable):

Who And/Or What Triggered Me   What Do I Forgive About The Past?
(Answer If Applicable)?

How Did I Respond To My Tigger Today   By Forgiving I Am:
(Answer If Applicable)?

How Did I Make My Trigger Powerless   Today I Stopped/Started/Maintained:
Today?

How Was I Present Today?   How Can I Retell The Story Of A Past
                                                Traumatic Event?

What Thoughts Did I Dwell On That I   I Let Go In Trying To Find The Answer/
Needed To Stop Thinking About That   Reason To:
Caused Unwanted Feelings?

Today I Realized: Tonight's Thoughts:

I Am Finding A Way To Leave It All Behind.

Made in the USA
Columbia, SC
23 September 2023

23204375R00152